The

MILITARISTIC
PROPHET'S

HANDBOOK

*A Comprehensive Guide to Understanding the Exceptional
Apostolic Leadership Appointment of the Classified Militaristic
Prophet's Mantle, Advanced Spiritual Warfare and Spiritual
Militaristic Operations*

TERESA MARTIN

TABLE OF CONTENTS

Acknowledgments 1

Introduction 3

Chapter One: What Is A (Spiritual) Militaristic Prophet? 9

The Militaristic Prophets' Mantle 9

The Role of The Militaristic Prophet 16

Gideon: The Short Order Militaristic Prophet 18

Characteristic of the Militaristic Prophet 19

Chapter One Review: 23

Chapter One Summary: 25

Prayer Strategy: 25

Chapter Two: The Making of The Militaristic Prophet 27

The Prerequisites 27

Conditioning and Training 32

The Militaristic Prophets Anointing 33

Seeing In The Spirit 34

Keen Discernment 35

Chapter 2 Review: 37

Chapter Two Summary: 39

Prayer Strategies: 39

Chapter Three: Spiritual Militaristic Operations 41

Operation Destiny 41

The System 48

Rescue Through Intercession 49

Rules for War 50

8 Core Instructions 51

Yah's Rescue Mission and Israel's Recovery 60

The Strategy to Obtain Deliverance 63

Psychological Warfare 66

The Breakdown 68

Chapter Three Review: 71

Chapter Three Summary: 73

Prayer Declaration: 74

Chapter Four: Militaristic Angels, Territorial Spirits and the Twice Dead 75

My Account with Angels 75

Mantle Protection 79

Under Orders 82

Generational Curses & Territorial Spirits 85

The Dead Twice and Divine Sentencing 87

Chapter Five: The Wartime Prophet 113

What is the difference between Wartime Prophets and Militaristic Prophets? 113

Daniel the Wartime Prophet 116

Serving Time 118

Chapter 5 Review: 120

Chapter Five Summary: 121

Prayer Strategy: 122

Chapter SIX: The Agent of Reformation 123

Nehemiah the Reformer 129

The Apostolic Mandate 131

Operation Lazarus 131

Chapter Six Review: 137

Chapter Seven: The Emerging Militaristic Prophet 139

A Letter to Militaristic Prophets 143

About the Author 145

ACKNOWLEDGMENTS

A great leader once said, "The only impossible journey is the one you never begin" ~Tony Robbins

When destiny calls you into service, your help will surely arrive. When the assignment to write this book was given to me, so were those who God would use to help bring the vision to pass. I would not have been able to do this without you. Your contribution to my life and this book will forever be appreciated. *~Teresa Martin*

Dexter Green Jr.

Ashlee Green

Sheryl Doby

Velina Jones

Taneka Thornton

Chanel Martin- WWM Family

Tonya Ratliff

My family and close friends

My present and former spiritual leaders

INTRODUCTION

Throughout the history of mankind, the call for true reformation has persisted. That initiative consistently evokes the call for the attributes engrained in the office of the Militaristic Prophet. One would think this particular title is a contemporary sector of the Army of God upon the earth. It's not. The Bible records centuries of battles and wars led by militaristic prophet's, exhibiting their conquests and defense strategies opposing hybrid enemy nations on Creator God's behalf. Moses, Joshua, Gideon, Deborah, Saul, David, and Samuel are all exemplary leaders utilizing the militaristic prophet's mantle in action during the return from exile and other deployments. While in exile, God positioned the Israelites to learn premier battle tactics from the most powerful military, belonging to the most powerful nation on the earth at that time: Egypt. This allowed the Israelites to receive unparalleled military training from God and man. The era of banishment God bestowed upon Israel was also used to prepare them to battle hybrid nations who were living in possession of the chosen nation's inheritance. It may be difficult to embrace, however, many authoritative bodies register as hybrid entities and are in some format of power today. Many of Israel's military assignments were to secure human resources and authority on the earth. Up until now the books containing Joshua's and Moses' account have been the most popular accounts discussed amongst biblical studies pertaining to warring with opposing nations to possess their God appointed land of promise. However, there are at least 10 wars recorded in the Bible that convey specific insight and instructions into understanding contemporary spiritual warfare. These wars gave Israel the ability to take back and consecrate their soul as a nation. The book of Joshua has several examples of war strategies and tactics given to anointed military leaders directly from God; showing the Israelites precisely how to take the land promised of their forefathers and overthrow the illegitimate governing powers ruling at that time. The nation of Israel was God's ideal government for His people during this particular time in history of man's process out of the state of the fall. The aforementioned 10 wars encompass God's promise to the forefathers of Israel. The blood that was shed on the cross at Calvary for the new covenant reveals the significance of those battle strategies and engagements as well as sets a new, higher standard for living and advancing the Kingdom of God on the earth. If you are a Prophet of Militaristic classification, it is in your best interest to study God's pattern for advancing in enemy territory. Without the proper training and Godly education, casualties of war will increase. The Church is in a state of emergence. The nations of the world are waking up to God's ultimate plan for humanity.

The reformers are coming. The reformers are here. The Militaristic Prophets' mantle is specifically designed to disrupt and disable demonic territorial spirits who are assigned to destinies and nations. Militaristic Prophets are gifted, mantled, and trained by the creator to reinforce and carry out God's specific plans for their assignments, and to subdue the ground. As these prophets complete their assignments they may procure various skills and obtain additional titles, such as: reformers, pioneers, trailblazers, world leaders, and scribes. Required tasks to be fulfilled during these assignments may include: shifting systems, unlocking destinies, uprooting territorial spirits, destroying strongholds, establishing the government of the Kingdom, as well as guarding and protecting annexed territories in the realm of the spirit until full manifestation. This Handbook is intended to serve you as a constant companion that will stimulate your courage and strengthen your heart; while delivering revelation knowledge and insight into divine master plans that will also serve to empower and treat your mantle as it relates to your calling. You will gain spiritual militaristic strategies and develop disciplines that will serve to position you in greater alignment with God's purpose and plan for your life. Unlike any other time in history, Militaristic Prophets are emerging with the fire and desire of the Lord's indignation and mercy. These prophets are fierce contenders for the faith, as they have been meticulously conditioned, trained, and processed. Their objective is to destroy demonic realities, dissolve demonic borders, expand, and hegemonize the Kingdom of God's rule on the earth. They possess unparalleled spiritual capacity and are developed as end-time warriors, apostolic agents, and defenders of the faith. As the new era advances, we will continue to see Prophets of Militaristic classification emerge of what appears to be out of thin air, and into every sector of society. I also think it's very important to note that this book is being birthed at the beginning of the end-time harvest and amid a revolution; a worldwide time of reformation. God promises a militaristic return to rescue His people from this current earth age. At the culmination of this age, He will come with thousands upon thousands of His saints in what appears to be a standoff.

Jude 1:14-15 NIV

[14] Enoch, the seventh from Adam, prophesied about them: "See, the Lord is coming with thousands upon thousands of his holy ones [15] to judge everyone, and to convict all of them of all the ungodly acts they have committed in their ungodliness, and of all the defiant words ungodly sinners have spoken against him."

This event is one the many reasons for much of the intense combat training we participate in and endure daily. Our meticulous trainings are militaristic on an optimum level. We are being groomed for the highest level of leadership available to God's descendants. This is how we will forever be known. You operate at the highest version of yourself through submission to Christ and the intense real time trainings He provides. God redeemed man for many reasons. There is a mind-blowing reality that awaits us in the future of humanity. God was redeeming that too. Periodically, my heart witnesses it in the spirit realm; however, my natural mind cannot comprehend the glory. What we write now will be in the "Library of the History of the Creation of the Earth". God in His justice will give full account to Himself for every timeline in History through the writings of His Prophets and scribes. These are "The Days of Redemption". What we are being commanded to write as inspired by the Holy Spirit will be a vast volume of chronicles of what will be known as the old world. What's in store for us after these seven prophetic days of creation and mankind's week long,

7-thousand-year introduction to history is over; is simply breathe taking. This book has been written to strengthen, inform, encourage educate, and transform the heart and mind of the reader. My prayer is that every Prophet of Militaristic classification would delve into the heart of these pages and stay in the vein. *"The weapons of our warfare are not carnal but mighty through God to the pulling down of strongholds, casting down imaginations and every high thing that exalts itself against the knowledge of God, and bringing every thought to the obedience of Christ." ²Corinthians Chapter 10:4– 5*

Grace to You,

Teresa Martin

Author of The Militaristic Prophet's Handbook

CHAPTER ONE

What Is A (Spiritual) Militaristic Prophet?

With an apostolic mandate, the Militaristic Prophet
is sent to establish territorial rule.
~Teresa Martin

Scripture Reference: *Joshua 1:2 NIV*

"Therefore, the time has come for you to lead these people, the Israelites, across the Jordan River into the land I am giving them."

The Militaristic Prophets' Mantle

As an authorized classification of the office of the Prophet, the Militaristic Prophet has an apostolic mantle. This mantle operates under mandates to restructure systems, tear down strongholds, uproots satanic structures, is deployed to Kingdom rescue missions and lay foundations that serve to advance the Kingdom of God in the earth. This office is also authorized and utilized on the stratospheric level. Once properly activated and treated, this Mantle moves through realms and dimensions undaunted. This mantled classification is authorized to release the judgment (good or bad) of the Most High upon its assignment with Heavenly reinforcement that has the capacity to baffle the world. Provided with an anointing for great leadership, God meticulously trains this officer against resilient, appointed oppositions to produce spiritual militaristic precision in the life of the office. Revelation knowledge exceeds the norm as this Mantle exists to eliminate carnal waste.

The assignments are rare. The opposition is fierce to say the least. This classification of the prophet's office contends with the forces of darkness ridiculously and continuously. Whether you are in traditional ministry, business, healthcare-whatever your field, understand that if you are mantled concerning this calling, you are called to the frontline. This Prophet is mantled for intense spiritual warfare! Great responsibility is given to this classified officer of the highest court.

Exceptional leadership is the key to exceptional outcomes. The quality of leadership rendered is dependent upon the level of personal sacrifice the purposed vessel is willing to provide. The level of training for maximum performance takes years to accomplish as proper training and conditioning are needed to develop the original intent. Courage is an essential leadership skill that sets the stage for the vulnerability that is needed to stabilize, connect influence, impact and develop organizations, families, corporations, and faith-based communities. This process grants the tools, language and skills to empower one to dominate their given sphere of influence. This chapter serves to highlight the innate qualities of this spiritual office-classification as well as give insight into the heart, disciplines and sacrifices that are unequivocally required to meet the standard of the calling in question.

Militaristic officers are often called to duty in the midst of crisis. They are specialized spiritual militaristic officers who are trained by Yah as spiritual warfare experts, trained to deliver beyond standard spiritual militaristic forces.

These trainings may include surveying amongst others. Often, Yah will send in one of His advanced highly skilled warriors into a covert operation. This is why you must be aware of the power of your silence. Moving in stealth mode should be second nature for you as you may need to gather required information and position yourself appropriately.

Trained under the mighty hand of God, this Prophet carries a very powerful influential presence that can shift cultures and climates with ease. Their demeanor can be misconstrued as stand offish or too deep. They can be widely misunderstood, due to the peculiarities of their mantle.

Exodus 33:11 NIV

"The LORD would speak to Moses face to face, as one speaks to a friend. Then Moses would return to the camp, but his young aide Joshua son of Nun did not leave the tent."

Joshua 3:7 NIV

"And the LORD said to Joshua, "Today I will begin to exalt you in the eyes of all Israel, so they may know that I am with you as I was with Moses.

With an apostolic mandate, the Militaristic Prophet is sent to establish and reinforce territorial rule. "

Joshua 1:2-5 NIV

"²Now therefore arise, go over this Jordan, thou, and all these people, unto the land which I do give to them, even to the children of Israel. ³ Every place that the sole of your foot shall tread upon, that have I given unto you, as I said unto Moses. ⁴ From the wilderness and this Lebanon even unto the great river, the river Euphrates, all the land of the Hittites, and unto the great sea toward the going down of the sun, shall be your coast. ⁵ There shall not any man be able to stand before thee all the days of thy life. "

The militaristic prophet operates with a measure of grace fit for a five star general. They are positioned on the frontlines of historical timelines such as, revolutions, wartime, the turnover of nations, leadership shifts, etc. They differ from wartime prophets as they are mantled commanders. We will discuss more concerning Wartime Prophets in chapter 7. Militaristic Prophets have a different spirit. They are ambitious visionaries and pioneers. They are relentless trailblazers who are wired to get to the finish line no matter the cost. When operating in their element they are unstoppable. These prophets are graced and trained to withstand spiritual foreign operations as they have an unusual courage about them. Fueled by the order of Heaven, these Prophets have a low tolerance for foolishness, sorcery, and sin. They have a no nonsense presence and are often misunderstood as they operate and speak from higher dimensions.

Joshua 1:1-9 NIV

"After the death of the Lord's servant Moses, the Lord said to Moses' helper, Joshua the son of Nun, [2]"My servant Moses is dead. So you and all these people get up and cross the Jordan River to the land I am giving to the people of Israel. [3]I have given you every place where the bottom of your footsteps, as I promised Moses. [4]Your land will be from the desert and from Lebanon as far as the big Euphrates River. It will be all the land of the Hittites to the Great Sea on the west. [5] No man will be able to stand against you all the days of your life. I will be with you just as I have been with Moses. I will be faithful to you and will not leave you alone. [6] Be strong and have strength of heart for you will bring the people in to take this land which I promised to their fathers to give them. [7] Only be strong and have much strength of heart. Be careful to obey all the Law which 'My servant Moses' told you. Do not turn from it to the right or to the left. Then all will go well with you everywhere you go. [8] This book of the Law must not leave your mouth. Think about it day and night, so you may be careful to do all that is written in it. Then all will go well with you. You will receive many good things. [9] Have I not told you? Be strong and have strength of heart! Do not be afraid or lose faith. For the Lord your God is with you anywhere you go."

Exodus 34:28 NIV

"Moses was there with the LORD forty days and forty nights without eating bread or drinking water. And he wrote on the tablets the words of the covenant--the Ten Commandments."

Militaristic prophets are YWHW's appointed Generals whose mantles are formed, fashioned- even activated by the very elements of warfare opposition sent to demolish their existence. Their mantles are treated in part by the climate of spiritual hostility; which is often tried and proven through immense heat. These mantels have been given a heavenly language, codes, symbols, and even dialect that concurs with the very blueprint of the mind of the Mighty Man of War; Jehovah Gibbor is His name.

Exodus 25:4 NIV

"See that you make them according to the pattern shown you on the mountain."

Acts of the Apostles 7:30-36 NLT

[30] "Forty years later, in the desert near Mount Sinai, an angel appeared to Moses in the flame of a burning bush. [31] When Moses saw it, he was amazed at the sight. As he went to take a closer look, the voice of the Lord called out to him, [32] 'I am the God of your ancestors—the God of Abraham, Isaac, and Jacob.' Moses shook with terror and did not dare to look. [33]"Then the Lord said to him, 'Take off your sandals, for you are standing on holy ground. [34] I have certainly seen the oppression of my people in Egypt. I have heard their groans and have come down

to rescue them. Now go, for I am sending you back to Egypt.'[35] "So God sent back the same man his people had previously rejected when they demanded, 'Who made you a ruler and judge over us?' Through the angel who appeared to him in the burning bush, God sent Moses to be their ruler and savior. [36] And by means of many wonders and miraculous signs, he led them out of Egypt, through the Red Sea, and through the wilderness for forty years. [37] "Moses himself told the people of Israel, 'God will raise up for you a Prophet like me from among your own people."

Militaristic prophets are weaponized through revelation knowledge that gives them the intelligence into what is normally concealed in the natural. They battle and rage with dark forces who are highly skilled and accomplished in their assignments to destroy.

Daniel 10:12-13 NIV

"Then he continued, "Do not be afraid, Daniel. Since the first day that you set your mind to gain understanding and to humble yourself before your God, your words were heard, and I have come in response to them. But the prince of the Persian kingdom resisted me twenty-one days. Then Michael, one of the chief princes, came to help me, because I was detained there with the king of Persia."

These officers elevate in rank through the ability to submit to a direct order in the midst of total chaos and confusion. We will cover the topic of carrying out direct orders in a later chapter. Not to be categorized with any other training, responsibilities or insight assigned of the average believer, this office classification is trained, mantled and assigned on a broader scope than the usual kingdom warrior. While both serve an important role in Kingdom affairs, the difference is as similar as a private in the military as oppose to a General. Militaristic prophets are provided Holy Angels whom are Elohim's spiritual military. These angles move in rank and file to accomplish what only the military of heaven can accomplish in the earth. We will discuss more about angelic assistance concerning this mantle in another chapter as well.

2 Kings 19:35 NIV

"That night the angel of the LORD went out and put to death a hundred and eighty-five thousand in the Assyrian camp. When the people got up the next morning--there were all the dead bodies!"

The Role of The Militaristic Prophet

In what we call the Old Testament, we can evidently see the spiritual Militaristic Prophets mantle in operation through Moses and Joshua, Deborah and a few others. In the New Creation Church, the role of the Militaristic Prophet hasn't changed much. However, it has been upgraded to meet the requirements of Gods New Creation family. Campaigns against the kingdom of darkness have been assigned and launched in stealth mode to accomplish the Kingdom agenda in the earth at full measure and discourse. These victorious campaigns can be and are often hidden behind the appearance of defeat. We can see evidence of this concept through analyzing the sacrifice at the cross of

Calvary. A trained spiritual militaristic eye can recognize the Militaristic Prophet's classification with ease. This classification carries a pioneering, trailblazing and reformation anointing. The opposition Militaristic Prophets undergo is fierce because many times they are assigned to groundbreaking feats. The territory in question is not only inhabited by illegal occupants and documents, these territories are contained and fortified by extremely hostile opponents with strongholds that only a militaristic mantle can take on. God has appointed believers in general to "Go into all the world." Many of these prophets have been on assignment under prophetic camouflage awaiting their next move to obtain total occupancy of the assigned ground. Some are awaiting deployment into ground that is currently being occupied by kingly demonic entities. These territorial princes are fully aware of their mantled opposition. As we see clearly through scripture, YWHW often uses the enemy's hidden works of darkness to accomplish His task. These prophets are often positioned in politics, the marketplace, the medical industry, the beauty industry, and any other arena hindered and controlled by demonic entities. They are placed in these arenas in order to bring about the reformation through the necessary weight of anointing to subdue demonic strongholds established by satanic systems and protocols. Militaristic Prophets thrive at breaking barriers. These prophets are given unique office classifications with an explosive mandated presence and anointing in the earth given by YWHW to enact the Kingdom. Again, this classification is typically groomed at birth, however, an individual can also be called on short order.

Gideon: The Short Order Militaristic Prophet

Full of fear, anxiety, doubt, and lack of confidence, Gideon was considered a simp when it pertained to war. He was from the weakest clan in the tribe of Manasseh, lacked courage and was void of certain understanding and faith concerning the things of God as it concerned Israel's battles. Short order Militaristic Prophets are ones who have not been trained since birth. They are abruptly pulled into action to fulfill the purpose of the Kingdom and may never be elected by God to operate in that function again. Scriptures suggest that Gideon was the greatest judge in Israel. However, he was a tepid, recreant man. He was found hiding on the threshing floor when the Midian's attacked and destroyed the nation's resources. So what was God's primary reason for drafting a man like Gideon to lead the army of Israel against the Midians? One very clear reason is located in 2 Corinthians 12:8-10, states that God's strength is made perfect in our weakness. It was clear that Gideon had no prior military experience, nor did he fully understand how God would use him to lead an army for the nation. At the time of his summons he lacked courage and the understanding of war strategies. Nonetheless, as Gideon stepped into his role as a government official, he obtained pivotal leadership skills while serving as a judge of Israel. His lack of experience coupled with his inclination to operate as a public servant, gave God the perfect opportunity to reveal His own sovereignty and strength over nations who were not of the commonwealth. God was able to show that at any given point in time He could quickly train, empower and mobilize a militaristic prophet to lead an army to victory on the behalf of Himself.

Characteristic of the Militaristic Prophet

The Militaristic Prophet's Mantle is unequivocally designed. This prophet's classification is groomed by Jehovah Gilbbor to be fearless in their engagement in ongoing battles with the forces of darkness and is upgraded, mentally, physically, and emotionally to do so. These battles are often prolonged, meticulous and rendered by the hand of God from birth. While every Blood bought believer engages in spiritual warfare, the Militaristic Prophet is called to the frontline and is fully capable to lead an army into victorious spiritual battles. They are born leaders, with a presence that is hardly unnoticeable. This classification is mantled and well equipped for mind boggling battles and misinterpreted victories.

Here are at least 65 characteristics to determine if you have the attributes of a Prophet of Militaristic classification or perhaps you are raising one or will serve with one in the future:

1) Tends to "see" demons from an early age.

2) May suffer abuse/torcher in early childhood

3) Experiences or have experienced physical assault with demonic agents

4) Unusual strong ability to "see" or sense the spirit world

5) Seems to be a target for witches and warlocks, attracts scorers, wizards, etc.

6) Tends to get in many fights at school

7) Enjoys (to a degree) physically fighting; doesn't mind confrontations

8) Tends to be fearless

9) First to confront an issue; they thrive in breaking barriers

10) Outspoken

11) Attracted to military precision and order

12) Orderly

13) Observant; detailed

14) Compassionate heart; despite all the other attributes

15) Has a deep need to understand given situations

16) Investigative spirit

17) Able to coordinate well during chaos and confusion

18) Excessive physical energy levels, (never seemed tired as a child)

19) Strategic in dealings

20) Always seem to be under unusual spiritual attacks

21) Innate ability to deduce likely scenarios

22) Advanced understanding of what looks like practical situations

23) Great measure of faith

24) Extremely risky and bold

25) Always standing up for someone else

26) Will fight for the underdog

27) Overly protective of loved ones

28) Have an unusual knowing of God from an early age

29) Understands they are "different "; a "loner"

30) Loves to obtain knowledge

31) Always seems to be the center of attention even when quiet

32) Very keen discernment

33) Able to carry a substantial amount of weight of glory through revelation

34) Very brave; unusually courageous

35) Physically stronger than their peers

36) Has a very deep need for God and a keen ear to hear

37) Can hear the boardroom of hell- satanic intel, plans and strategies

38) High mental ability for solving problems

39) Low tolerance for sin, foolishness and lack of order

40) Powerful unforgettable presence

41) Authoritative personality and demeanor

42) Tends to live from the onside out; same outfits for months are the norm for this mantle as they are very artistic and tends to progress in alignment of the weather and, or spiritual moods and movements in the earth

43) Very creative

44) Somewhat high maintenance personality

45) Lives in constant transitions

46) Pretty much stay in conflict

47) Strong desire to accomplish great things

48) Are attractive to the spirit realm whether good or bad; paranormal realm, wraith/phantom spirits, witches, angels, extraterrestrial beings, etc.

49) Loves mysteries and conspiracy theories

50) Are often tormented by bad dreams, spiritual/physical assaults during sleeping

51) Are targeted by witches, demons, negative people

52) You have the feeling that odd and, or negative things that tend to happen in your life has something to do with you; their presence. But you feel you can't put your finger on it. (Hint, it's your warfare)

53) You feel like they have a knowing and understanding about things you should not normally know about-

54) Photographic Memory; remember things, event others don't. Early childhood as early as one or two years old, etc.

55) Usually targeted by tragedy after tragedy even if small in comparison to some

56) As a child- always in the most "trouble"

57) Very strong personality

58) A rule breaker

59) A rescuer at heart

60) Can't stand the thought of defeat; will finish the race even if they must crawl to the finish line.

61) High level imagination can tell stories or describe the event using clear picture story telling skills

62) Will NOT give up or quit under pressure

Chapter One Review:

1) What is the Spiritual Militaristic Prophet?

The Militaristic Prophet is YWHW's advanced duel functioning apostolic reinforcement officer in the earth. This officer works in full collaboration with military angels who move in rank and file to accomplish what only the military of heaven can accomplish.

2) What is their primary assignment?

To establish an advanced Kingdom, territory on the earth, and to pave the way for the Kingdom of Heaven to be hegemonized on earth. They are assigned to destiny assignments and must adhere to strict obedience as they are usually assigned to destinies.

3) Why is the opposition against the Militaristic Prophets mantle so fierce?

This is because this classification carries a trailblazing, pioneering, and anointing.

Their opposition is fierce because many times they are assigned to groundbreaking feats. The territory in question is not only inhabited by illegal occupants and documents, these territories are contained and fortified by extremely hostile opponents with strongholds that only a militaristic mantle can take on.

4) How are Militaristic Prophets weaponized?

They are weaponized through revelation knowledge that gives them the intelligence into what is normally concealed in the natural. They battle rage with dark forces who are highly skilled and are accomplished in their assignments to destroy the works of darkness.

5) What are some of the characteristics of the Militaristic Prophet?

See, Characteristic of the Militaristic Prophet

6) How do they fit into the New Creation Church?

The Militaristic Prophet's Mantle has been upgraded to meet the requirement of the 21century Church. They are positioned in various realms of influence; mantled for total occupancy.

Chapter One Summary:

The Militaristic Prophets is a unique office classification with an explosive mandated presence and anointing in the earth given by YWHW to enact Kingdom. Great responsibility is given to this officer of the highest court. Trained under the mighty hand of God, this Prophet carries a very powerful influential presence. These have been given heavenly language, codes, symbols, even dialect that concurs with the very blueprint of the mind of the Messiah, Christ. This officer elevates in rank through the ability to submit to a direct order while during chaos and confusion. Not to be categorized with the given responsibilities and awards assigned of the average believer, this office classification is trained, mantled and assigned on a broader scope than the usual kingdom warrior. While both serve an important role in Kingdom affairs, the difference is as similar as a private in the military as oppose to a General.

Prayer Strategy:

Lord of all, you have provided me with strength, wisdom, understanding, knowledge, and power to move strategically in the earth according to the measure of faith in which we are measured. You have mantled me according to you perfect plan for humanity. I thank you for granting me a greater understanding concerning your purpose for my life and I am in full agreement, allegiance, and alliance with all that it entails. You have mantled me according to your purpose- your will be done on earth as it is in Heaven, unto the glory of the Father of Spirits. I ask that you would release an increase of your seed of revelation within me and cause it to burst unto the fullest manifestation of your glory that you've created and capacitated me to reveal. Grant me exceptional skill and abilities as you granted Daniel that will gain me the necessary resources that pertain unto life and Godliness as you have provided to maximize Kingdom influence in the earth. I bless you as you continue to train the Kingdom warrior within me as I position and keep my soul purified by obeying the truth. Glory to God - so be it.

CHAPTER TWO

The Making of The Militaristic Prophet

❧

Our mental warfare is allowed to Militarize the
mind against satanic intrusions
~Teresa Martin

Scripture Reference: Joshua 1:8 KJV

"This book of the law shall not depart out of thy mouth; but thou shalt meditate therein day and night, that thou may observe to do according to all that is written therein: for then thou shalt make thy way prosperous, and then thou shalt have success."

The Prerequisites

There are specific prerequisites required concerning this distinguished classification. A person who is called to carry such a heavyweight of authority, anointing, and revelation must endure vast demonic exposure; sometimes even before stepping into the relationship with the Son that reveals the calling. God orchestrates situations and circumstances that outlines specific training that this prophet classification will need during their spiritual militaristic career. Witches, warlock, spells, pacts, seals... nothing is exempt! Before I accepted the calling to the office, I was exposed to demonic encounters of what seemed to be every kind. Without my knowing, God exposed me to very high-level spiritual warfare, much of what is not addressed in this day and time amongst the Body of Christ. I was trained in very hostile territory and had been battling highly intense and heavily saturated, satanic witchcraft unbeknownst to me for most of my life. Witchcraft works on different levels. While I do not condone any form of divination, it is important to note that witchcraft has different levels of intensity; ranging from what appears to be harmless to the practitioner and those around them, to life altering and life threating to all who come in contact with them. Trust and believe they are not all redeemable by the blood. I know that made some of you stop in your tracks, but some know exactly what I'm talking about. Nevertheless, this state of being exists. There are those who walk the earth and are apostates. The book of Jude calls them the "twice dead". They roam the earth as vagabonds. I encourage reading more about this fallen state in the book of Jude for further individual research. Throughout this book, as I give account of the first-hand encounter with this type of being, I will make reference to them as "the witch."

Ephesians 6:12 NIV

"For our battle is not against flesh and blood, but against the rulers, against the authorities, against the world powers of this darkness, against the spiritual forces of evil in the heavens."

Training concerning these dimensions, realms and divisions were stratospheric in measure. Meaning, they were elevated battle grounds that served to condition me for the next dimension of my calling- the awakening. I discuss these matters in later chapters. I was given a front row seat to a stratospheric generational satanic assignment concerning a family whose bloodline was targeted by specific destiny altering spirits by way of ancient rituals, that resulted in generational curses. Generally speaking, the assignment was to kill steal and destroy, but the focus was to create a bloodline that would bring forth desecration and multiply Satan's descendants in the earth. During the last few years of my life prior to giving my life to God, I started dating someone who introduced me to "the witch" and her family. One of the first things she (the witch) asked me was "Are you saved?". At that time I was unaware that demons could spiritually identify those who *will* inherit salvation.

Hebrews 1:12 NIV

"Are not all angels ministering spirits sent to serve those who will inherit salvation?"

My immediate answer was, "yes". This was because at that time, I thought that simply knowing that Christ was the Son of God meant you were "saved". Back then, I prayed every now and again and had a constant knowing that God was always with me, however, I didn't have a real relationship with Christ. I had not been regenerated yet. The Holy Spirit taught me A LOT through that experience. In a later chapter I will give an account concerning this very eye opening testimony of what the word of God refers to as "the twice dead". Take note,

Satan is obsessed with having his own bloodline in the earth. He has many children here now. Everyone you see in a body is not necessarily, or even 100% human. Some theological studies suggests that it is possible that Cain was not from Adams bloodline at all. He is not mentioned in the genealogy reference anywhere in the word of God. However, the book of James says,

James 3:12 NIV

"Do not be like Cain, who **belonged** to the evil one and murdered his brother. And why did he murder him? Because his own actions were evil and his brothers were righteous."

Jude 1:12 NIV

"These people are blemishes at your love feasts, eating with you without the slightest qualm--shepherds who feed only themselves. They are clouds without rain, blown along by the wind; autumn trees, without fruit and uprooted--twice dead."

It turned out that this particular witch had a grandmother who was also a witch. Her assignment was to produce and train offspring to carry the satanic legacy. These are called hereditary pacts and seals. Hereditary pacts and seals are covenants and sealants that are applied to the patriarchs and matriarchs of a family. They are strategically targeted to recruit the entire family through these covenants and sealants. The Lord revealed that the grandmother made these heredity pacts and seals with Satan concerning the familial bloodline. Because of that, he will always come after them. He believes they are his. I designed and teach a class about this practice called Pacts and Seals at Militaristic Prophets Institute. The Holy Spirit revealed to me that this particular family is kept under watch by what is called *advanced satanic concentrations*. The witch of this particular family would tell me stories about why she was no longer able to seek the Lord. I couldn't understand why she would say such a thing, when even at that time considering my lack of spiritual knowledge, I knew that God would never leave nor forsake his people. I wasn't aware of the vagabond spiritual status. I had no knowledge of the twice dead nor did I know that she provoked the Lord to anger, repeatedly and aggressively, unto the point of court martial unto death. She had been shown much mercy, but she did not receive it and continued in the ways of her flesh. I'll explain more about that later.

Advanced satanic concentrations are strategically assigned to those who are assigned to the nations. An example of such would be the life of Prophet Daniel. Daniels assignment in ancient Babylon did not appear to be militaristic in nature. He wasn't assigned to lead an army out of bondage or into the land. However, Daniel was mantled for politics. Herein, his militaristic mantle showed up expressing great integrity and excellence in his battlefield. His account of the fierce battle that took place in the heavens revealed his rank and stature, as it would be illegal for demonic opposition to rank higher than its target. The principle of rank exists in every realm. These battles concerning Daniel's request for such a weighty understanding were stratospheric in measure. The angelic host who was assigned to deliver the message was met head-on with a principality assigned to a human king. I'd say that ranks pretty high. A satanic concentration assignment provides the surveillance and data needed to infiltrate as it is used to hijack God's purpose for one's life by way of the assignment to utterly destroy.

Conditioning and Training

Routine betrayals, exceedingly harsh environments, (what looks like) lack of stability in this prophet's life can all be seen and misinterpreted as failure to those who watch from near and far. The warfare is immense to say the least. Day after day the militaristic prophet is trained against unusual onslaughts that would be considered unbearable to the average believer. The life and mantle function of this classified prophet is activated under great pressure. This pressure is designed to delete the ego and advance the tactical and strategic skillset of the prophet, by applying divine fire that reshapes the structure of their mindset and DNA. This classification, depending on the calling, rank, and assignment will find their training full of psychological disputes that includes mental onslaughts that eventually enhances and upgrades their mental acumen and spiritual gifts. Without the grace of God dispensed and at work in the life of this prophet, survival of the daily drills, tests, break downs and build ups would not be an option. We are able to see this in the life of Moses. Upon the awakening of his heart concerning his people while he served in Egypt, he quickly removed himself from pharaoh's wrath after he murdered an Egyptian overseer. He then found himself living a life that appeared to be one of absolute defeat. In the eyes of the Egyptians, a Shepherd was viewed as repulsive. Again, Yahweh grooms this classification through the harshest conditions. A life of transition is not unusual, while this prophet is being made a powerhouse, fortified city, and an absolute nightmare to the kingdom of darkness. Grooming for this classification is different for each individual because every calling and assignment is different. Some militaristic prophets are protected from warfare as a child, others are molded and shaped through great warfare, resistance, and mind bending torments. What I'm saying in this portion of this book is not intended to provoke fear within you; but to empower and enrich your life through revelation; understanding, knowledge and wisdom concerning your mantle and mandate or that of a loved one.

The Militaristic Prophets Anointing

The militaristic prophets anointing creates an extraordinary and unusual life for its carrier. It gives them the spiritual ability and agility to walk through doors, take flight, and soar beyond your general life expectations. The anointing elevates above concrete situations and allows one to dwell amongst people who would've been unreachable without it. It produces the necessary weight of glory to provide for the most effective leadership, influence, insight, affluence, and success in the most difficult situations. An anointing for breakthrough is associated with this mantle as the militaristic prophet's anointing is specifically formulated to bring liberty to its assignment. This mantle also brings utter destruction to obstacles (mental yokes and burdens) that plagues people, families, businesses and nations. The anointing empowers and enriches the life of its carrier. The preparation process to produce such a genuine, powerful life transforming flow of oil on one's life is often described as excruciating. This anointing agitates dark forces on extreme levels. The sacrifice is immense as it includes years, even decades of preparation that also includes a heavy dose of humiliation, domino setbacks, epic financial loss, biblical style visions and revelations, immense frustration, epic transitions, routine betrayals, delays, time loss, dramatic disappointments, rejection on steroids, and excessive spiritual warfare. As well, it provides mind blowing visitations from the Lord and His Holy Angels, unparalleled fellowship, and revelation knowledge that will fill the temple with the Glory of God. This specific anointing is formulated and shelved for a specified amount of time to produce a very valuable, rare, weighty, precious commodity made accessible in the earth through an extremely submitted vessel.

Seeing In The Spirit

The revelation knowledge afforded to this mantle is spectacular to say the least. The visitations from the God-head are indescribable. One would think this prophet was delusional when sharing the visions and experiences afforded to this prophet's classification. In the service of his/her training there is great backlash from those who secretly oppose the truth. Once early on in ministry, I was harassed by a fellow believer who was said to have made phone calls to churches in the city telling them to disregard the teaching concerning spiritual warfare I was facilitating at the time. She spoke of how I was teaching the "doctrine of demons". Mind you, this was before she'd ever heard any of the teachings. Needless to say, many were delivered, strengthened, and confirmed and her misguided view of my mantle served to backfire concerning her own credibility in the realm of the spirit. This "sister" decided that it was her job to "watch" every move I made. Her submission to such diabolical council opened her up to backlash from the very demons she so ignorantly entertained. You see, her deliverance was in my mouth and she spoke against it. We all know that Satan is an accuser of the brethren. It's simply his job to discredit the messengers of the Gospel of Christ. Unfortunately, sometimes believers will make themselves available for his usage. This is why deliverance is fought and needed. When someone is not delivered, it makes them available to dark forces for maximum usage. It's important to know that the mantle of the militaristic prophet is nothing to take lightly. One can set themselves back years through positioning themselves against this purpose. A rare authority and anointing rest upon this mantle. This Prophet receives early in ministry, assignments that stretches them to the core. The daily amount of intense spiritual warfare can sometimes be described as "ridiculous". Once I was speaking to spiritual officer (a respected prophetess), and during the conversation she said, "Your daily warfare would make the average believer want to commit suicide". I took a closer look to my life and the many, many challenges that I was facing on the daily basis at that time and decided she was probably right. I must admit that I needed to reevaluate the statement. Due to the tremendous dispensation of the grace of God poured upon my life, suicide is never an option. God is truly faithful to His children.

Keen Discernment

Militaristic Prophets have innate spiritual gifting's. Hearing very clearly in the realm of the spirit is one of them. During the time of my prerequisite training I was able to hear commands being given sporadically. Generally, they take on the form of thoughts, but actually they are utterances that can be heard (in the spirit-mind) throughout any given realm of influence. These types of utterances can be assigned by the witch or warlock designated to abolish the purposed vessel before salvation is received in the earth or to overthrow an assignment that is already in the works. Targeted from birth, there always seemed to be some kind of battle going on over my presence. It seemed as though no matter who was in the room, I somehow always ended up being the center of attention. Needless to say, it was a drag. It always made me feel uncomfortable. Later on in life after I gave my life to the Lord, I began to understand that the mantle that God had placed upon me (before the foundations of the world) would attract demonic attacks with the intent to overthrow God's purpose for my life and those I'd be called to serve. It also qualified me for great personal protection though God would allow the mantle to be authenticated through great trials as it is this day. What I didn't know then was that there was a keen gift of discernment within me that gave me an unusual awareness of whatever was behind the scenes in the room. As a child, there were just things I knew without being told. A very keen gift of discernment accompanies this classification and serves as proverbial high tech radar pertaining to its realm of influence and assignments. I came to understand that this gift annoys dark forces to the third degree. They absolutely hate the exposure.

Fast forward by the age of 14, I would wake up to my bed shaking in the middle of the night. Having been living in Los Angeles, California, I naively thought that there was an earthquake every night until I found out it wasn't. I know, I know, that was pretty naive. I was well acquainted with the spirit of fear as a blasphemous spirit use to sit in the corner of my room, speak evil declarations over me while staring at me and eluding the feeling of fear simultaneously. What I didn't know was that the spirit that was there to intimidate me, was intimidated itself. I never asked myself why I always saw in the spirit realm, nor could I articulate that it was the spirit realm that I was seeing into but I did. I saw and had a knowing of many things, even out of my immediate surroundings.

Chapter 2 Review:

1) **What is the name of those who are apostate in the earth and wonder like vagabonds?**

   There are those who walk the earth and are apostate, they are called the "twice dead." You can read more about this fallen state in the book of Jude.

2) **Why is Satan obsessed with having his own bloodline in the earth?**

   He wants to be like YWHW Elohim. He has many here in disguise and desires to fill the earth with his offspring to continue his legacy.

3) **What is a hereditary pact and seals?**

   Hereditary pacts and seals are covenants and sealants that are applied and made by the spiritual patriarchs and matriarchs of a family. These types of families are kept under watch by what is called advanced satanic concentrations.

4) Why is the spiritual warfare for the militaristic prophet so immense?

The life and mantle function of this classified prophet is activated under great pressure. This pressure is designed to delete the ego and advance the tactical and strategic skill set of the prophet, by applying vast heat that reshapes the structure of their DNA. This classification-depending on the calling, rank and assignment will find their training full of psychological disputes that includes mental onslaughts that eventually enhances and upgrades mental acumen and spiritual gifts. Without the grace of God dispensed and at work in the life of this prophet, survival of the daily drills, test, break downs and build ups would not be an option.

5) Are all militaristic prophet's trained the same?

Grooming for this classification is different for each individual because every calling and assignment is different. Some militaristic Prophets are protected from warfare as a child some are molded and shaped through great warfare, resistance and mind bending torments.

6) What does the militaristic prophet's anointing provide for the carrier?

It elevates above concrete situations and allows one to dwell amongst people who would've unreachable without it. It produces the necessary weight of glory to provide the most effective leadership, influence, insight, affluence and success in the most difficult situations. An anointing for breakthrough is associated with this mantle as militaristic prophets anointing is specifically formulated to bring liberty to its assignment, while bringing utter destruction to obstacles (mental yokes and burdens) that plagues people, businesses and nations likewise while empowering and enriching the life of its carrier.

Chapter Two Summary:

The revelation knowledge afforded to this mantle is spectacular to say the least. The visitations from the God-head are indescribable. One would think this prophet was delusional when sharing the visions and experiences afforded to this prophet's classification. The preparation process to produce such a genuine, powerful life transforming flow of oil on ones' life is often described as excruciating. This anointing agitates dark forces on extreme levels. Day after day the Militaristic Prophet is trained against unusual onslaughts that would be considered unbearable to the average believer. The life and mantle function of this classified prophet is activated under great pressure.

Prayer Strategies:

Lord of Glory, power and authority belongs to you. I exist for and by you as you are the author and finisher of my faith and the King of my heart. Because of you I can leap over walls and withstand any and every opposing force. Your ways are majestic and righteous. Your power is unmatched. While the battles that are afforded to me come to prove my mantle, your great and unsearchable love confounds the works of darkness that seeks to destroy me. Truly, there is no one like you. Thank you for providing for yourself in the earth- a yolk destroying, burden removing anointing that pierces the darkness, sets the captives free and causes me to live according to you standard. Take our relationship to greater heights and deeper depths according to your tender mercy and your great grace. You are God alone. I yield to your perfect plan for my life. Thank you for continued access through the Word the Blood and the Holy Spirit.

CHAPTER THREE

Spiritual Militaristic Operations

'Militaristic Prophets are not only called to frontline spiritual war-fare; they are called to aggressively take back ground. This is done through Kingdom legislation, intercession and prophetic enactments concerning the rescue and recovery of spiritual POW's as well as to retrieve encroached land in the realm of the spirit".
-Teresa Martin

Scripture Reference Exodus 3:7-8 NIV

"[7] The Lord said, "I have indeed seen the misery of my people in Egypt. I have heard them crying out because of their slave drivers, and I am concerned about their suffering. [8] So, I have come down to rescue them from the hand of the Egyptians and to bring them up out of that land into a good and spacious land."

Operation Destiny

The Church is yet to fully see the splendor of Moses' delegated assignment against Pharaoh as a spiritual militaristic operation. In fact this was a recovery operation. The name denotes the nature. Moses was born during a time that the Egyptians were enacting government sanctioned genocide against the Hebrews. This was a wartime tipping point for the distressed nation. Militaristic prophets are often born, introduced and/or elevated into their sphere of influence in a time of elevated chaos, confusion and war. They have a heart for justice and will answer with courage. Ancient literature records Moses' meticulous military training and it is evident in the way he responded to the Lords command to go back to Egypt on a rescue mission to deliver the nation from the grips of their enslavement. Moses was reluctant to obey Gods command because He had been previously trained in the Egyptian military, who at that time in history was the most powerful nation on the face of the earth. Take note, it is the military coverage, the power that come with it and wars won at turning points in history that gives a nation their notable reign and claim to dominance. Moses understood this and was hesitant to embrace the order proceeding out of the mouth of the Lord even while being revealed through the dramatic introduction to His Majesty via burning bush.

Exodus 3:10-15 NLT

"[10] So now, go. I am sending you to Pharaoh to bring my people the Israelites out of Egypt."[11] But Moses said to God, "Who am I that I should go to Pharaoh and bring the Israelites out of Egypt?" [12] And God said, "I will be with you. And this will be the sign to you that it is I who have sent you: When you have brought the people out of Egypt, you will worship God on this mountain." [13] Moses said to God, "Suppose I go to the Israelites and say to them, 'The God of your fathers has sent me to you,' and they ask me, 'What is his name?' Then what shall I tell them?" [14] God said to Moses, "I am who I am. This is what you are to say to the Israelites: 'I am has sent me to you.'" [15] God also said to Moses, "Say to the Israelites, 'The Lord the God of your fathers—the God of Abraham, the God of Isaac and the God of Jacob—has sent me to you. [16] "This is my name forever, the name you shall call me from generation to generation. "

Clearly Moses was not excited about going back to Egypt. He knew how hard it would be to conquer the nation in question because of his experience in leading campaigns in regards to the nation's conquest. As a former member of the Royal First Family of Egypt, his training was rigorous and he knew firsthand what the Egyptian military was capable of. His reluctance to return to his homeland was born of fear and fueled by experience. Moses was content with his new life. Being banished in the backside of the desert didn't seem so bad compared to facing Pharaoh. I can imagine the mental preoccupation ion his mind concerning his people in Egypt. Your destiny and calling will tug on your heart all your life and if you don't answer, and you will always be dissatisfied until you step into it. So, beware, procrastination can cause you to run out of time and there's no sting quite like regret.

Moses plead with the great *I AM* about choosing someone else. Surely, someone with more charisma or good speaking skills could face Pharaoh instead. After all, he was an exiled member of the royal family and extremely self-conscious of his speech impairment.

Exodus 4:17 NIV

"Moses answered, "What if they do not believe me or listen to me and say, 'The LORD did not appear to you'?"

² Then the LORD said to him, "What is that in your hand?" "A staff", he replied. ³ The LORD said, "Throw it on the ground." Moses threw it on the ground and it became a snake, and he ran from it. ⁴ Then the LORD said to him, "Reach out your hand and take it by the tail." So Moses reached out and took hold of the snake and it turned back into a staff in his hand. ⁵ "This," said the LORD, "is so that they may believe that the LORD, the God of their fathers—the God of Abraham, the God of Isaac and the God of Jacob—has appeared to you." ⁶ Then the LORD said, "Put your hand inside your cloak." So Moses put his hand into his cloak, and when he took it out, the skin was leprous—it had become as white as snow. ⁷ "Now put it back into your cloak," he said. So Moses put his hand back into his cloak, and when he took it out, it was restored, like the rest of his flesh. ⁸ Then the LORD said, "If they do not believe you or pay attention to the first sign, they may believe the second. ⁹ But if they do not believe these two signs or listen to you, take some water from the Nile and pour it on the dry ground. The water you take from the river will become blood on the ground." ¹⁰ Moses said to the LORD, "Pardon your servant, Lord. I have never been eloquent, neither in the past nor since you have spoken to your servant. I am slow of speech and tongue." ¹¹ The LORD said to him, "Who gave human beings their mouths? Who makes them deaf or mute? Who gives them sight or makes them blind? Is it not I, the LORD? ¹² Now go; I will help you speak and will teach you what to

say." **13** But Moses said, "Pardon your servant, Lord. Please send someone else." **14** Then the LORD's anger burned against Moses and he said,
"What about your brother, Aaron the Levite? I know he can speak
well. He is already on his way to meet you, and he will be glad to see
you. **15** You shall speak to him and put words in his mouth; I will help
both of you speak and will teach you what to do. **16** He will speak to
the people for you, and it will be as if he were your mouth and as if
you were God to him. **17** But take this staff in your hand so you can
perform the signs with it."

Under no circumstances was Moses confident enough to jump in head
first to confront Egypt concerning giving up there financial well-being
through bringing liberty to their wealth generators, the Hebrew slaves.
Moses demonstrated his military training and expertise physically and
psychologically through the execution of an Egyptian before his flight
out of his residence and service of the nation. Not only did he kill the
Egyptian with ease, scripture doesn't indicate that he had any remorse,
or hesitation concerning the murder. This can be explained by having
to carry out orders to kill while in the service to Egypt's military. It
also revealed his heart attitude towards the Egyptians tyranny. Moses'
actions revealed his drive to defend and protect his people from the
injustice, affliction, and brutality that is a result of slavery. This also
categorized him as a social reformer. It revealed his militaristic state
of mind towards his opposition. Notice that Pharaoh never gave an
order for Moses to be locked away or killed. This of course, was the
Lords doing. However, Moses had a reputation concerning the many
victorious campaign feats that were won in his historic time of military
leadership. Pharaohs underline respect for Moses' presence revealed

that. The function of Moses' mantle is evident through hair raising miracles. Ranging from a bloody Nile river, to a plague of frogs and gnats, to the ultimate destruction of Pharaohs immediate bloodline through the death of his first born, who was the heir to the throne. He was crowned with the responsibility to deliver the nations constitution, laws, and to be the mediator of the first covenant sprinkled with blood at the mountain of Sinai after spending a total of 80 days and 80 on the mountain without food or know water.

Moses was told by God to stretch forth his rod and tell the children of Israel to move forward, after asking Him, "Why are you calling on me?". This was a new place of authority and activation for Moses as scripture reveals that he was unsure of the next move to make while standing at the boarder of the sea. God showed Moses a new level of authority due to his obedience which involved authority over the waters in the earth as well as put to bed the idol worship concerning a water-god that was worshiped in Egypt.

Exodus 24:8-18 NIV

[8] Moses then took the blood, sprinkled it on the people and said, "This is the blood of the covenant that the LORD has made with you in accordance with all these words." [9] Moses and Aaron, Nadab and Abihu, and the seventy elders of Israel went up [10] and saw the God of Israel. Under his feet was something like a pavement made of lapis lazuli, as bright blue as the sky. [11] But God did not raise his hand against these leaders of the Israelites; they saw God, and they ate and drank. [12] The LORD said to Moses, "Come up to me on the mountain and stay

here, and I will give you the tablets of stone with the law and commandments I have written for their instruction." [13] Then Moses set out with Joshua his aide, and Moses went up on the mountain of God. [14] He said to the elders, "Wait here for us until we come back to you. Aaron and Hur are with you, and anyone involved in a dispute can go to them." [15] When Moses went up on the mountain, the cloud covered it, [16] and the glory of the LORD settled on Mount Sinai. For six days the cloud covered the mountain, and on the seventh day the LORD called to Moses from within the cloud. [17] To the Israelites the glory of the LORD looked like a consuming fire on top of the mountain. [18] Then Moses entered the cloud as he went on up the mountain. And he stayed on the mountain forty days and forty nights.

The power of the blood offers divine protection and serves to unite spiritually and legally. Rahab entered into a blood covenant with Israel through the mission of the spies. She had a twofold covenant with them. They made a verbal agreement then she sealed her faith destiny decision with the scarlet cord. Elohim had set the standard and made a blood covenant offering protection within the fibers of the destined nation's existence, coupled with an agreement concerning the mission.

This is true covenant. Blood-contract authorized and signed with the breath of agreement. Rahab and her family were good to go. This not only insured her survival, but the survival of her bloodline as she was engrafted into the bloodline of Christ through David by faith. It is important that you understand weapons that are used for destiny operations. Faith releases you from death to life.

The System

Moses served as no threat to Pharaoh as long as he was in service to Egypt. While Egyptian slavery represents bondage, Babylonian slavery represents assimilation. We must remember that Egypt was the most powerful nation on the earth at that time. Much of their military power protected a system they created in order to become the greatest. As a matter of fact, the military was a part of that system. While it is not recorded in scripture, it wouldn't be above Pharaoh to have been given understanding concerning the prophesy of a deliverer who was supposed to bring the chosen nation out of exile. One could say that he was hidden in the system in order to never be able to identify with his true identity. On the contrary, God had placed him in the system in order to overthrow it at the appointed time. Pharaoh understood the system in which an Egypt existed. Moses embodied the system. They made Moses one of the many the strengths of Egypt. They assimilated the Hebrew child. This was because they wanted to make sure that Egypt lived within him. He made sure Egypt was engrained into Moses' heart in order to ensure that Egypt would never be destroyed. You cannot break out what you don't know exist! So when Moses awakened to his purpose Pharaoh tried to kill him. Why? Why try to kill one that you raised up on purpose? Because Pharaoh knew that Moses had understanding of the system. Moses' display of empathy turned to anger, showed pharaoh that his mind had broken free and now he had become Egypt's greatest threat. A freed mind is an enemy to an oppressive environment. Pharaoh was now probably the head of the military. God appeared to play yo-yo with pharaoh's will concerning the matter of deliverance. Jehovah Gilbbor is His name.

Rescue Through Intercession

There are various types of rescue missions. Some are designed for high profile destiny recovery and some are general in measure. High profile rescue missions are dramatic in nature and will usually be branded in history as a supernatural occurrence. These missions are so extraordinary there will always be a question of their authenticity. In prophetic rescue missions, the calling of intercession is key. Without proper intercession, the mission could never be completed.

Journaling is mandatory. There must be a daily account of what is brewing in the spirit realm in order to steward the prophetic word over the mission to avoid delay or complete mission abortion. Your journal is considered your wartime journal. A healthy diet of the Word of YHWH, daily fellowship with His Majesty and daily communion is the foundation of the victory of the assignment. This is not as easy to carry out as it sounds. These basic instructions require a level of discipline that will bring forth the measure of authority necessary to fulfill the mission. A successful outcome will take total submission. Intercession elevates your discernment and gives you the capacity to hear, feel, taste, and see what is being concealed by optical illusions-cast from dark forces. Through official Kingdom mandated intercession, you are seated concerning the ground. This means heaven has authorized your full authority to rule the ground under submission to His lordship. Authority empowers your mandate. You are given the grace, the favor, the mindset, and the necessary resources to complete the assignment. There will be times of stretching, warring, death, standing, creating, resting, battling blatant sorcery, and sitting during your assignment through intercession. You will receive strategies for battle, feel in tuned emotions, hear conversations, and more in order to gain the ability to navigate through the realm in question.

Rules for War

When it comes to winning spiritual battles, there are always regulations that must be adhered to. These specific directives are put in place by God and are needed to provide order to ensure a successful outcome. There are also regulations and commands that become relevant once your entry into your promise is manifested.

Deuteronomy 18:9–14 NIV

9 "When you come into the land that the Lord your God is giving you; you shall not learn to follow the abominable practices of those nations. 10 There shall not be found among you anyone who burns his son or his daughter as an offering, anyone who practices divination or tells fortunes or interprets omens, or as sorcerer 11 or a charmer or medium or a necromancer or cone who inquires of the dead, 12 for whoever does these things is an abomination to the Lord. And because of these abominations the Lord your God is driving them out before you. 13 You shall be blameless before the Lord your God, 14 for these nations, which you are about to dispossess, listen to fortune-tellers and to diviners. But as for you, the Lord your God has not allowed you to do this."

No matter what the situation or battle looks like, God is always fighting for you. It would literally be impossible for you or me to win the types of battles we are designated to without the instructions and help from the Elohim of all the earth. Elohim gives clear instruction about what is required upon entering into the land of promise. These regulations and guidelines are centered around His holiness and meet the requirements He desires. Keep in mind these nations that were being evicted were hybrid humans. There could be no way to defeat another species without the absolute power of Elohim backing them and no way to continue to occupy the realm if you choose to worship their Gods in the midst. You likewise contend daily with hybrid mindsets, businesses, situations, circumstances, cultures, and people. I've listed eight basic core instructions that will serve to help you develop a greater measure of discipline and give greater clarity and understanding concerning strategies and tactics you can use in order to stay in momentum, even if you are exhausted from the resilience training.

8 Core Instructions

1. Receiving Divine Instructions For The Battle Is Mandatory

Your mantle does not give you permission to move out of the perimeters of your assignment. Failure to submit to the protocols of your assignment can result in severe unbearable backlash and sometimes death. You MUST go before Adonai to gain sufficient understanding concerning your portion of the assignment. Yahweh has a plan. A blueprint. He doesn't make things up as you go, nor is He surprised by the urgent situations in your life. He always has your best interest in mind and promises absolute victory.

2. Obedience Is Key To Victory

Israel was brought low in the eyes of the people who would gain word of their victories when they fail to FULLY obey God's covenant instructions before going to battle with the Moabites. According to the meal covenant, there should've been a burnt offering presented according to the ordinance of the meal covenant. A burnt offering indicated that there would've been a blood/animal sacrifice that morning that would have served to cover Israel during the battle. Their disobedience brought public shame to them even in the midst of a victorious battle. The blood sacrifice of the king could only work if his blood offering was greater. Israel won the battle but they were taken back due to the King of Moabite sacrifice of his own son. His act of sorcery released a stigma against the destined nation that should not have been the results of a victory backed by God and well won. This is why you must study the battle plays provided in the first covenant. They are valid today as it pertains to operating in the realm of the spirit. It has been brought to my attention the absolute necessity of taking communion every morning and every evening. Sure, I can apply the blood of the Lamb by faith, but communion was instituted by Yeshua on the night He was betrayed. He successfully covered the meal offering portion of Gods divine constitution, laws and protocols through the last supper. As we participate daily with this spiritual application of discerning and taking part of His blood and body, we are operating in a core component of the covenant. Participating in this practice also blocks all word curses, plans of general demonic intent, and the effects of demonic blood sacrifices made by assigned witches and warlocks to hinder and/or overthrow the plans and purpose of the assignment. The sacrifice of the Lamb of God provides us the ability to apply the blood where necessary. Daily communion reinforces the power of the Blood of the Lamb in the earth.

2 Kings 3:24-27

24 But when the Moabites came to the camp of Israel, the Israelites rose up and fought them until they fled. And the Israelites invaded the land and slaughtered the Moabites. 25 They destroyed the towns, and each man threw a stone on every good field until it was covered. They stopped up all the springs and cut down every good tree. Only Kir Hareseth was left with its stones in place, but men armed with slings surrounded it and attacked it. 26 When the king of Moab saw that the battle had gone against him, he took with him seven hundred swordsmen to break through to the king of Edom, but they failed. 27 Then he took his firstborn son, who was to succeed him as king, and offered him as a sacrifice on the city wall. The fury against Israel was great; they withdrew and returned to their own land.

You are sealed unto the day of redemption. A literal blood transfusion has redeemed your soul as the life (soul) is in the blood. But be aware and obey promptly. It is not abnormal for demonic host to use the principle and supreme reality of blood (generally speaking) to bind and hinder the souls of unsuspecting men. This causes delay in destiny and many time ultimate destruction of one's destiny which is nothing short of catastrophic. Selah.

Watch what you eat in the natural and in the spirit. The soul is altered through eating and sexual intercourse. *(See the Book of Leviticus)* What you believe will alter your soul too. What you believe can bind you or liberate you. There are only two choices, life or death. There are demonic soul binding, perversion tactics that serves to anchor God's chosen through the lust of the flesh, the pride of life and the seeing of the eyes. May your comprehension concerning such things expand in the 'Holy Spirit'. You will not perish because of lack of knowledge. May every iron-clad, spellbinding tactic be severed in your life in Yashua's (Jesus') mighty and matchless name. His Blood is superior.

3. Be Resilient.

Quitting is not and will never be an option. You are trained on an optimum level and that requires stripping you until you are the intended structure. People can be born with the attribute of resiliency and groomed as well. The greater the passion you carry about your purpose, the greater the opposition will be in the assignments you are tasked with. These forces of opposition will do everything in their power to keep you from fulfilling your assignments. Resiliency shows God that you can be trusted with greater responsibility. It is the tenacity that can be trusted. Resistance is our best friend. Because of it, we obtain the muscle to walk upon the high hills of the earth. By it we are strengthened in our resolve. Resilience is produced by the affliction assigned to the purpose. Every assignment that is rendered to you should be taken seriously and treated with the highest priority.

Psalms 18:33 NIV

³³ He makes my feet like the feet of a deer; he causes me to stand on the heights.

Psalms 119:71 NIV

⁷¹ It was good for me to be afflicted so that I might learn your decrees.

You are a militaristic spiritual agent. Your calling will never be comfortable. However, you have a measure of grace that gives you the ability to survive the pressure meet with the superiority of a submarine. You were built by Elohim to last. Humility is your assignment.

Esther 2:5-7 NIV

⁵ Now there was in the citadel of Susa a Jew of the tribe of Benjamin, named Mordecai son of Jair, the son of Shimei, the son of Kish, ⁶ who had been carried into exile from Jerusalem by Nebuchadnezzar king of Babylon, among those taken captive with Jehoiachin⁽ᵃ⁾ king of Judah. ⁷ Mordecai had a cousin named Hadassah, whom he had brought up because she had neither father nor mother. This young woman, who was also known as Esther, had a lovely figure and was beautiful. Mordecai had taken her as his own daughter when her father and mother died.

4. Steward the Prophetic Word And The Mission Well

Journaling is underrated and is essential to actualizing the victory of a battle. It gives you an outline of the strategies to implement as well. It will keep you in a place of awareness which is essential to the victory in the battle. When you fulfill your duty to write, you are providing future generations with wartime playbooks and journals inspired by the Holy Spirit. Your descendants will appreciate the insight, as Daniel did as he was able to read Jeremiah's writings and govern himself. This tool keeps the truth of history recorded in the earth. It's always bigger than you think.

Daniel 9:2 NIV

[2] "In the first year of his reign, I, Daniel, understood from the Scriptures, according to the word of the LORD given to Jeremiah the prophet that the desolation of Jerusalem would last seventy years.

Joshua 18:8 NIV

[8] "As the men started on their way to map out the land, Joshua instructed them, "Go and make a survey of the land and write a description of it. Then return to me, and I will cast lots for you here at Shiloh in the presence of the LORD."

5. Circumcision

Studying the Word is non-negotiable. Without it you will not have the strength, courage, or mindset to complete the assignments. Do not allow yourself to drift off. These words were written to help us navigate our journey. You must have staying power, because dark forces will do everything possible and promotable to destroy you before you enter in.

Their assignment is to wear you down via domino effect in order to get you to let down your faith shield. Remember, dark plans for you are so low in value it would take years to accomplish. This is why self-inventory/circumcision of the heart is a perpetual requirement.

Romans 12:2 KJV

And be not conformed to this world: but be ye transformed by the renewing of your mind, that ye may prove what is that good, and acceptable, and perfect, will of God.

6. Map Out Your Assignment

Spy out the land by what you see in the spirit realm. Before you enter into your promised land, God will prepare you spirit, soul and body. Just remember, it is possible not to be ready when you enter in. There may be some consequences to that. God prepares you for your task by healing you and shifting your paradigm pertaining to your assignment. This is usually because by the time it is time to truly enter into the land, you've had a few false alarms, misinterpreted time frames, and severe disappointments. Heck, the promise itself may be betting against you. However, as you yield in intercession to your new place of submission to the negbw, you likewise are being prepared through that same assignment as you intercede through the assignment. Your submission to what can be the harsh reality of the road to recovery is what will recover you as well. Take note, if someone has left your life and they return without the Lord going before them and making the crooked places within you straight as far as dealing with you concerning them, then usually they weren't sent. Keep a distance until you receive instructions. Then with detail, write them down.

7. Be Quiet

Your silence can be used as a weapon. You cannot trust everyone with the blueprint of His Will for your life. Be mindful of repeated questions coming from those who really don't understand your walk. Sometime dark forces will use a trusted relationship in order to extract information from within. Ask the Holy Spirit to show you the informants in your life. They serve as opened portals to the kingdom of darkness and will position themselves as a detriment to you and your mission. Some have no idea that they are being used and some do. Govern yourself accordingly.

James 1:9 NIV

[19] Know this, my beloved brothers: let every person be quick to hear, slow to speak, slow to anger:

8. Rest

Another expedient ingredient that gives balance to your assignment is rest. We are commanded to rest! Early in mantle activation I experienced some training which included a lack of sleep or continuous harassment from dark forces. Sometimes depending on the territorial spirits, prior achievements, and the level of your training, you may even experience physical warfare such as: spontaneous attacks, physical ailments, or outburst from a susceptible host. Expecting this kind of hostility can be extremely overwhelming, but do not fret. These are all given to move you into a new place of authority as you are being groomed for promotion after promotion unto your expected end. If you find yourself feeling engulfed by the fierce continuous opposition you should take 1-2 full rest days where you purposeful do absolutely nothing! If you haven't been doing this or you find yourself feeling guilty for taking the day off, you may need to remind yourself on those days that you deserve rest. You deserve peace. Also, keep in mind that rest is actually productive! So, if you experience guilt for doing nothing and taking a break, remember you are actually doing something extremely important: resting. Ask God to reveal the second day to you as the Sabbath (Saturday) should be honored as God intended. Be gentle with yourself. God is for you and wants to replenish you.

2 Corinthians 4:16 NIV

16 "Take my yoke upon you and learn from me, for I am gentle and humble in heart, and you will find rest for your souls".

2 Corinthians 5:17 NIV

17 "Repent, then, and turn to God, so that your sins may be wiped out, that times of refreshing may come from the Lord."

Yah's Rescue Mission and Israel's Recovery

Militaristic prophets are given classified spiritual intelligence that serves to demolish the temporary rule of territorial spirits. Their mantle provides the ability to carry out the assignment that serves as a blueprint and grants eventual unhindered access into naturally concealed spiritual territories, realms, and dimensions. For example, Joshua was mantled to secure freedom, scribal writing, given authority over the sun, and distributing the allotment over territories. More examples of Joshua exercising his God given mantle are in the scriptures as follows:

Joshua 6:1-27 NIV

[1]Now Jericho was straightly shut up because of the children of Israel: none went out, and none came in.

[2] And the Lord said unto Joshua, See, I have given into thine hand Jericho, and the king thereof, and the mighty men of valor. [3] And ye shall compass the city, all ye men of war, and go round about the city once. Thus shalt thou do in six days? [4] And seven priests shall bear before the ark seven trumpets of rams' horns: and the seventh day ye shall compass the city seven times, and the priests shall blow with the trumpets. 5) And it shall come to pass, that when they make a long blast with the ram's horn, and when ye hear the sound of the trumpet, all the people shall shout with a great shout; and the wall of the city shall fall down flat, and the people shall ascend up every man straight before him. 6) And Joshua the son of Nun called the priests, and said unto them, Take up the Ark of the Covenant, and let seven priests bear

seven trumpets of rams' horns before the ark of the Lord.[7] And he said unto the people, Pass on, and compass the city, and let him that is armed pass on before the ark of the Lord. [8] And it came to pass, when Joshua had spoken unto the people, that the seven priests bearing the seven trumpets of rams' horns passed on before the Lord, and blew with the trumpets: and the ark of the covenant of the Lord followed them. [9] And the armed men went before the priests that blew with the trumpets, and the reward came after the ark, the priests going on, and blowing with the trumpets. [10]And Joshua had commanded the people, saying, Ye shall not shout, nor make any noise with your voice, neither shall any word proceed out of your mouth, until the day I bid you shout; then shall ye shout. [11] So the ark of the Lord compassed the city, going about it once: and they came into the camp, and lodged in the camp. [12] And Joshua rose early in the morning, and the priests took up the ark of the Lord. [13]And seven priests bearing seven trumpets of rams' horns before the ark of the Lord went on continually, and blew with the trumpets: and the armed men went before them; but the rearward came after the ark of the Lord, the priests going on, and blowing with the trumpets. [14] And the second day they compassed the city once, and returned into the camp: so, they did six days. [15] And it came to pass on the seventh day that they rose early about the dawning of the day, and compassed the city after the same manner seven times: only on that day they compassed the city seven times. [16] And it came to pass at the seventh time, when the priests blew with the trumpets, Joshua said unto the people, Shout; for the Lord hath given you the city. [17] And the city shall be accursed, even it, and all that are therein, to the Lord: only Rahab the harlot shall live, she and all that are with her in the house, because she hid the messengers that we sent. [18] And ye, in any wise keep yourselves from the accursed thing, lest ye make yourselves accursed, when ye take of the accursed thing, and make the camp of Israel a curse, and trouble it. [19] But all the silver, and gold, and vessels of brass and iron, are consecrated unto the Lord: they shall come into the treasury of the Lord. [20] So the people shouted when the priests blew with the trumpets: and it came to pass, when the people heard the sound of the trumpet, and the people shouted with a great shout, that the wall fell down flat, so that the people went up into the city, every man straight before him, and they took the city. [21] And they utterly destroyed all that was in the city, both man and woman, young and old, and ox, and sheep, and ass, with the edge of the sword. [22] But Joshua had said unto the two men that had spied out the country, go into the harlot's house, and bring out thence the woman, and all that she hath, as ye swore unto her. [23] And the young men that were spies went in, and brought out Rahab, and her father, and her mother, and her brethren, and all that she had; and they brought out all her kindred, and left them without the camp of Israel. [24] And they burnt the city with fire, and all that was therein: only the silver, and the gold, and the vessels of brass and of iron, they put into the treasury of the house of the Lord. [25] And Joshua saved Rahab the harlot alive, and her father's household, and all that she had; and she dwelleth in Israel even unto this day; because she hid the messengers, which Joshua sent to spy out Jericho. [26] And Joshua adjured them at that time, saying, "Cursed be the man before the Lord that riseth up and buildeth this city Jericho: he shall lay the foundation thereof in his firstborn, and in his youngest son shall he set up the gates of it." ²⁷ So the Lord was with Joshua; and his fame was noised throughout all the country.

Joshua 5:13-15

¹³ And it came to pass, when Joshua was by Jericho, that he lifted up his eyes and looked, and, behold, there stood a man over against him with his sword drawn in his hand: and Joshua went unto him, and said unto him, Art thou for us, or for our adversaries? ¹⁴ And he said, "Nay; but as captain of the host of the Lord am I now come. "And Joshua fell on his face to the earth, and did worship, and said unto him, "What saith my Lord unto his servant?" ¹⁵ And the captain of the Lord's host said unto Joshua, Loose thy shoe from off thy foot; for the place where-on thou standest is holy 'In every sector of society'.

This office is dispatched by exceptional leadership and they legislate the rescue and recovery of spiritual POWs' in the realm of the spirit. Their capacity for revelation knowledge emanating from the Throne Room of heaven is impeccable.

The Strategy to Obtain Deliverance

God heard the cry of the nation of Israel to be delivered. He heard their cry the same way He hears your cry and the cry of those He assigns you to. Upon His answer, He began to shift the heart of Moses; a deliverer whom He'd already placed in the nation as a seed for a sure harvest at the appointed time. Moses had to be delivered from the trappings of Egypt. Likewise with you, there are many things you've been through as yokes and bondages are called against the ministry of deliverance. You may have found yourself delivered into bondage against your will or through no fault of your own, only to be delivered out in due time in order to gain the authority and training needed to administer deliverance to others. The level of density associated with this move is remarkable. Daniel, Shadrack, Meshack, and Abednego, were Hebrew exiles in Babylon who at some point after enduring many previous trials were put into the furry furnace. What is sometimes overlooked in this passage of scripture is the fact that they had to qualify for that level of trial. Meaning, they would've had to be eligible to withstand a trial of that magnitude, which would only come through previous trials of great magnitude. The dual function of a trials and refining of faith is often overlooked. First, there is qualification to go to the next realm and dimension in glory. Then, there is the aftermath of that measure of purification operating in the earth. A promotion follows a purifying fire such as the one the three young, Hebrew boys endured. God is a Mighty Man of War. Jehovah Gibbor is His name. His strategy to deliver the children of Israel entailed meticulous tactics, counter attacks, psychological warfare among other calculated warfare methods. He targeted Israel's fierce opposition through attacking their economy through various means. The 10th plague was one that ensured that Pharaohs line of succession would be cut off as the mass militaristic operation began to come to full mission achievement. It is not widely known, but after the God of Israel's demonstration of power against ancient Egypt they were never again considered a world power. In this we see deliberate means for destruction to be brought upon the hostile nation by the God of Israel. God's strategy was to send Moses to request a three day leave to go into the wilderness to worship. But His overall plan was to deliver them completely from the consequences of their disobedience and to bring them out with great substance.

Exodus 7:3-4 NKJV

³ And I will harden Pharaoh's heart, and multiply My signs and My wonders in the land of Egypt. ⁴ But Pharaoh will not heed you, so that I may lay My hand on Egypt and bring My ⁱᵃˡarmies *and* My people, the children of Israel, out of the land of Egypt by great judgments.

Exodus 11:1 NIV

¹¹ Now the LORD had said to Moses, "I will bring one more plague on Pharaoh and on Egypt. After that, he will let you go from here, and when he does, he will drive you out completely. ² Tell the people that men and women alike are to ask their neighbors for articles of silver and gold." ³ (The LORD made the Egyptians favorably disposed toward the people, and Moses himself was highly regarded in Egypt by Pharaoh's officials and by the people.)

Sorcery is currently running rampant in the world as well as the Church. When a Militaristic Prophet is assigned to a rescue mission they are immediately exposed to witchcraft. One of many ways sorcery is used is to disguise bondage. It is also used deceive those who are subject to its purpose. When Moses was sent back to Egypt to deliver the Children of Israel, he met Pharaohs witches, sorcerers and magicians. Friend of God, He calls you to penetrate the stronghold. More often than not there is always an illusion casted as an assignment involving the rescue mission of a POW(s). Every plague represented a certain god that was held in high esteem in Egypt.

Exodus 7:1 NIV

Then Pharaoh called in his own wise men and sorcerers, and these Egyptian magicians did the same thing with their magic.

God chose to speak to Pharaoh up close and personal by targeting his vain, reprobated faith in the abominable gods; whom deflated in their influence in-light of the God of Israel's highly publicized destiny rescue mission. Israel, under the leadership of Joshua would go on to win countless battles against territorial assigned hosts and possess the land of promise, even as they received their allotment.

Psychological Warfare

While God was breaking Pharaoh down psychologically, He was simultaneously restoring Israel's faith back in Him. We must understand the psychological impact that captivity has on the captives. Israel lived in captivity for roughly 430 years. While they desired freedom, their minds had already been conditioned to the ways of Egypt. This is evident in their response to the patience God was rebuilding in them by way of deliverance and provision.

Numbers 11:5 NIV

[5]We remember the fish which they ate freely in Egypt, the cucumbers, the melons, the leeks, the onions, and the garlic.

Keep in mind that a mindset precedes a mandate. While leaving exile, Israel needed to see every movement played out by their God. The crossing over the waters represented the cleansing of the nation and the washing away of their old life in Egypt. Now they were set in motion; upon what should have been a short time of travel and training concerning their new assignment and conquest. Full delivery was witnessed firsthand by the chosen nation. But they had been psychologically damaged and conditioned to question their own value and worth. They had been trained to operate with a "tail" mindset within the wicked camouflaged nation. The nation who had been delivered by the God of Israel through the intercession of Moses now needed to be made free in their minds with the end in mind that they would enter into their destiny. As you receive assignments from the Lord understand that regardless of what it looks like on the outside, the rescue target is in a state of imprisonment by way of sentencing either by direct or indirect spiritual violations. Many times the rescue target is so engulfed in deception they are not even aware that they need to be rescued. But don't worry, later is coming. They are often warned repeatedly concerning pending destruction due to deliberate disobedience. Often these POWS' have been court marshaled as a result of dishonoring a direct order from God. When this happens, they usually have been sentenced by Heaven's Supreme Court and will be processed in that realm until released to fulfill their destiny. There will be much required of you as you are court appointed to fulfill a mandated rescue mission. You will pay great personal price to fulfill your destiny but it will be worth it! Moses received intelligence from the mouth of the Lord directly. The Word of God records that Moses spoke to God face to face. This mirrors a Commander in Chief speaking face to face to a five star general.

The Breakdown

Exodus 8:28 (NIV)

[28] Pharaoh said, "I will let you go to offer sacrifices to the Lord your God in the wilderness, but you must not go very far. Now pray for me."

"Now pray for me". This request from Pharaoh revealed his state of mind, as God was using the plagues to break down his mental strength. More than likely, Pharaoh obtained this level of mental endurance due to his superior military training and conditioning. This was the fourth plague. Pharaoh was on his last leg at this time. Keep in mind that Pharaoh's upbringing included Egyptian education (sorcery and dark arts) and military training. So God knew that his heart and mind was able to bounce back after being torn down because it had been trained and conditioned that way. Herein the Lord was operating as the ultimate Commander in Chief. Consider Pharaohs narcissistic boasting and bragging concerning himself and his aspiration concerning the future of the great nation. It is clear that the Lord was exercising His power and authority over what was deemed the most powerful nation in the earth.

Exodus 8:28-32 NIV

28 Pharaoh said, "I will let you go to offer sacrifices to the Lord your God in the wilderness, but you must not go very far. Now pray for me." **29** Moses answered, "As soon as I leave you, I will pray to the Lord, and tomorrow the flies will leave Pharaoh and his officials and his people. Only let Pharaoh be sure that he does not act deceitfully again by not letting the people go to offer sacrifices to the Lord." **30** Then Moses left Pharaoh and prayed to the Lord, 31 and the Lord did what Moses asked. The flies left Pharaoh and his officials and his people; not a fly remained. 32 But this time also Pharaoh hardened his heart and would not let the people go.

Now during the sixth plagues of boils the Word of God records that "God hardened Pharaohs heart". By this time Pharaoh had been compromised psychologically. God proceeded to take further total control of the situation by breaking Pharaoh down and hardening his heart again to rebel. God has the ability to tap into and restructure the psychological pattern of any willing or unwilling individual. He begins working on your heart concerning any people, place, or thing in order to break down the current reigning stronghold. Often our confession is the artillery that is needed to cause walls to fall or destruction to be thwarted. Dark forces fight this aggressively. The strategy is to wear you out mentally and emotionally with resistance. Any word that is spoken out of obedience is usually the necessary spiritual explosives deemed necessary for infiltration of the encroached land.

The walls of Jericho were constructed to keep intruders out. These walls were fortified by demonic rituals, tissues from aborted babies, and were rumored to be built by Nephilim (human- fallen/angels hybrids). It is said that the walls were so thick that a Calvary of horses could run on the top of them and the walls were fully supported in structure. This operation reveals the horrendous battles the militaristic mantle is ordered to take on. Prophets of militaristic classification are called to contend with demons specified through militaristic classification as well. This also speaks of the rank and orders of assignment. The power that is accompanied by the military of the Kingdom's angelic host grants absolutely victory over every assignment pertaining to dark forces. When God wanted to deliver Israel out of the bondage of slavery He moved in meticulous order and strategy. This is not about perfection; this is about precision that is a result of total submission. Whenever there is new assignment being delegated to you, there will also be witchcraft. Militaristic Prophet, you will always be summons to deal with high ranking witches. They are no one to be afraid of. They are often assigned to high ranking Kingdom officials. God may use the attack to train you for battle; however they are defeated through your submission to Christ. Militaristic Prophets are usually targeted by principalities all their life. This positions them to be in spiritual battles long standing, sometimes continuously. The spirit of witchcraft will often use the Word of God to manipulate those they target. Indeed, the spirit of Jezebel is vain, divisive, and narcissistic in personality. Those who make themselves available to demons will not prosper without repentance. Some of these are never able to return.

Chapter Three Review:

1. How did Moses' response to the God of Israel's summons to go back to Egypt reveal the hidden purpose of his reluctance?

Ancient literature records Moses' meticulous military training and is evident in the way he responded to the Lords command to go back to Egypt on a rescue mission to deliver the nation from the grips of their enslavement. Moses was reluctant to obey Gods command because He had been previously trained in the Egyptian military who at that time in history was the most powerful nation on the face of the earth. Take note, it is the military coverage, the power that come with it and wars won at turning points in history that gives a nation their notable reign and claim to dominance. Moses understood this and was hesitant to embrace the order proceeding out of the mouth of the Lord even while being revealed through the dramatic introduction to His Majesty via burning bush.

2. What are the rules for war?

When it comes to winning spiritual battles, there are always regulations that must be adhered to. These specific directives are put in place by God and are needed to provide order to ensure a successful outcome. There are also regulations and commands that become relevant once your entry into your promise is manifested.

Deuteronomy 18:9–14 NIV

3. What are the eight core instructions?

1) Receiving Divine Instructions

2) Obedience is key to victory

3) Be resilient

4) Steward the prophetic Word and the mission well

5) Circumcision

6) Map out your assignments

7) Be quiet

8) Rest

4. How are militaristic Prophets equipped for rescue missions?

Militaristic Prophets are given classified spiritual intelligence that serves to demolish the temporarily rule of territorial spirits as well as the ability to carry out the assignment that serves as a blueprint and grants eventual 110 unhindered access into naturally concealed spiritual territories, realms and dimensions. Joshua was mantled to secure freedom, scribal writing, and authority over the stratosphere, distributing the allotment over territories, etc.

5. How does Elohim use the militaristic Prophets mantle concerning witchcraft/sorcery?

Sorcery is currently running rampant in the world as well as the Church. When a Militaristic Prophet is assigned to a rescue mission they are immediately exposed to witchcraft. One of many ways sorcery is used is to disguise bondage. It is also used deceive those who are subject to its purpose. When Moses was sent back to Egypt to deliver the Children of Israel, he met Pharaohs' witches, sorcerers and magicians. Friend of God, He calls you to penetrate the stronghold. More often than not there is always an illusion casted before an assignment involving the rescue mission of a POW(s).

6. What happens after a militaristic prophet has been consistently, unrepentantly and deliberately disobedient to Elohim?

They are often warned repeatedly concerning pending destruction due to deliberate disobedience. Often these POWS' have been court marshaled as a result of dishonoring a direct order from God. When this happens, they usually have been sentenced by Heaven Supreme Court and will be processed in that realm until released to fulfill their destiny.

Chapter Three Summary:

Militaristic Prophets are not only called to frontline spiritual warfare, they are called to aggressively take back ground and legislate the rescue and recovery of spiritual POW's in the realm of the spirit. Their capacity for revelation knowledge emanating from the Throne Room of heaven is immaculate.

This mantle will always have to contend with witchcraft and destiny altering spirits. They are assigned to destiny operations and are meticulously trained to do so.

Prayer Declaration:

Father, I thank you for entrusting me with assignments that are so precious to you- the souls your people. You have granted me access that only you can give. Thank you for those you will rescue in you tender mercy and great grace. Great is your mercy. I agree with your perfect plan for humanity as I grow in grace and the excellence of your council. Thank you for rescuing me; that I may be used by you to intercede for others however you choose. May your deliverance be recurved from those you have granted and may our hearts continue to yield to your voice. So be it!

CHAPTER FOUR

Militaristic Angels, Territorial Spirits and the Twice Dead

❦

"If you are mantled for the nations there is a demon prince that is assigned to hinder your ability as there was with Daniel. As well, a chief prince assigned to you to defeat your fierce opposition". You've been granted a seat as it pertains to your legal jurisdiction.
-Teresa Martin

Scripture Reference: Daniel 10:20

"So, he said, "Do you know why I have come to you? Soon I will return to fight against the prince of Persia, and when I go, the prince of Greece will come.""

My Account with Angels

I can remember my first account with Angels in my teenage years. These encounters mostly took place in the middle of the night. I would wake up suddenly like we all do, just consciousness in between the dream world and the physical world. I would hear what I knew to be two Angels speaking about me to each other. I could only hear a glimpse of their conversation. Through their voices, I could see their tall, and heavily built forms. Their faces were an enigma to me. As they closely faced each other, they spoke simultaneously concerning me. Neither of them waited for the other to finish speaking, as these angels could speak to one another concurrently, without confusion. They communicated very differently from how humans verbally communicate. As they spoke to one another, I could hraer that they were speaking in a tongue not from this Earth. I understood that they were highly conscious of me and on one occasion, I knew they were discussing plans to protect me. I heard these beautiful, powerful, Angelic beings on several occasions throughout those years.

1st Corinthians 13:1 NIV

"Though I speak with the tongues of men and of angels, and have not charity, I am become as sounding brass, or a tinkling cymbal."

When Angels show up they sanctify the ground. They bring with them the atmosphere of Heaven. They show up by way of command, sent under God's authority to provide insight, understanding, provision, defense, and protection. They are gentle, yet fierce and ready for battle. They are orderly as they move in rank and file.

The Joshua 5:13-15 NIV

13 "Now when Joshua was near Jericho, he looked up and saw a man standing in front of him with a drawn sword in his hand. Joshua went

up to him and asked, "Are you for us or for our enemies?" [14] "Neither," he replied, "but as commander of the army of the Lord I have now come." Then Joshua fell facedown to the ground in reverence, and asked him, "What message does my Lord[e] have for his servant?"

[15] The commander of the Lord's army replied, "Take off your sandals, for the place where you are standing is holy." And Joshua did so.

Some years back, I was working in the medical field caring for a couple in their home and one of my clients was in the hospital for surgery. It was my off day, payday, and I was speaking to a sister in Christ over the phone at the time of my arrival to the hospital. I was still in the car when in a moments time; I began to feel the atmosphere shift. Holiness now ruled the climate and I saw in the spirit realm, Angels descending from Heaven. The parking lot was full of them. Immediately I got off the phone and began to worship. It was literally all that I could do. I carefully inquired of the Lord if there was any danger. I did that because I knew that they had come from His presence and had been deliberately sent to me. I knew they were on assignment personally for me. But why so many? I though in my natural mind for a minute "Maybe there's a gunman around, what's happening"? as My spirit man continued to worship. I inquired the Lord again and He began to speak to me concerning my client. Apparently, this man had a mantle that called forth massive divine protection in a life threatening situation. The Lord began to show me that there were witches in the hospital who would sabotage his recovery, thus the Kingdom assignment that was designated to me. These witches would also be able to recognize my mantle and assignment towards my client. I strongly understood that he needed spiritual and natural protection. The angels were sent that day to me as well, as I later found out that my client was adamant about maintaining his staff, primarily me because of the shift, to aid him privately outside of the hospital staff. I saw how Angelic presence warded off excessive demonic activity in that hospital. When God has a prophetic assignment concerning your life, He will protect you from death until then. Weeks later, I was on shift the night my client returned to his home. That night my spiritual ears witnessed a fight going on in the garage and in the living room. This battle was between holy angels and fallen angels for this man's life. I prayed and made declarations and decrees of life and peace; superimposing and reinforcing Gods plans continuously. One night several months before he passed on; I was working the night shift as usual and I dosed off for a bit. My eyes suddenly popped open and I saw a demon with an ancient, greenish breastplate standing in the hall staring at me. I knew this was a demon of generational curses. I knew it had walked a bloodline. I knew that this particular spirit had been connected to the bloodline of this family since WW2. God revealed to me that there was inheritance at stake in the realm of the spirit. There was something this generational spirit had been warring over for a long time. There had been some injustices, but they must answer to the blood of the Lamb of God. Be mindful that your spiritual inheritance usually includes the convergence two different bloodlines to bring forth. Your spiritual inheritance flows directly from the mind of Christ, which the heart of God's plan with the intent to bless and fulfill His plan for humanity.

Mantle Protection

The militaristic prophets mantle provides an undetermined level of divine Angelic protection to the purpose and destiny we carry. They minister to the war-torn.

1 Kings 19:5-8 KJV

"And as he lay and slept under a juniper tree, behold, then an angel touched him, and said unto him, Arise and eat. [6] And he looked, and, behold, there was a cake baked on the coals, and a cruse of water at his head. And he did eat and drink, and laid him down again."[7]And the angel of the LORD came again the second time, and touched him, and said, Arise and eat; because the journey is too great for thee. [8] And he arose, and did eat and drink, and went in the strength of that meat forty days and forty nights unto Horeb the mount of God.

When militaristic prophets have been called to a certain battle their Angelic counterpart shows up to mark the territory in question. They not only assist in the battle, they ensure the victory. They can be sensed, seen, felt and heard. The passage below gives us the ability to see the scale of their assignments and commitment to the battles we are assigned to.

Joshua 5:13-15 NLT

[13] "Now when Joshua was near Jericho, he looked up and saw a man standing in front of him with a drawn sword in his hand. Joshua went well up to him and asked, "Are you for us or for our enemies?" [14]

"Neither," he replied, "but as commander of the army of the Lord I have now come." Then Joshua fell facedown to the ground in reverence, and asked him, "What message does my Lord[e] have for his servant?" **15** The commander of the Lord's army replied, "Take off your sandals, for the place where you are standing is holy. And Joshua did so."

Pay close attention and take note of the capacity of your battles. They give you a glimpse into the scope of your assignments, anointing, and influence. Throughout scripture we have witnessed Angelic host as warriors, messengers, ministers, defenders, and rescuers. The tenth chapter of Daniel gives us an account of a battle that took place in the heavenly realm between two high ranking Angels, Michael and the demon prince, who was sent to hinder the delivery of revelation concerning a vision eventually delivered from Gabriel, to Daniel. The messenger Angel by the name of Gabriel, was contending with the demon prince connected to the king of Persia. This is because both the king of Persia and Daniel were both classified Militaristic Prophets/Apostles positioned and connected to the destiny of a Israel to play their part in unveiling this epic, celestial battle. We must remember that gifts and calling are irrevocable. The king or ruler of a nation is also the commander in chief- the head of the military of that particular nation. Daniels assignment in Babylon offers another perspective concerning the realms of influence, mantle duties, practices, provisions, anointing and grace provided for the militaristic prophets' mantle and assignment.

Daniel 2:48-49 NIV

[48]"Then the king made Daniel a great man, and gave him many great gifts, and made him ruler over the whole province of Babylon and chief of the governors over all the wise men of Babylon." [49] "Then Daniel requested of the king, and he set Shadrach, Meshach, and Abednego, over the affairs of the province of Babylon: but Daniel sat in the gate of the King."

God positioned Daniels's mantle, anointing and purpose as second in command as it relates to His own sovereignty over the nations. The measure of favor upon his mantle was extraordinary. Daniel led the military of Heaven in the earth byway of His mantle in his realm of influence. Daniels's position gave God the legal access that was needed to govern Israel while exiled in the earth. God does all things in order. Through Daniels faithfulness and dedication, God was able to have an official Kingdom mantled representative in the political realm to bring His influence through Daniels's life and the life of those who belonged to Him. In other words, God had mercy on Israel. His submission positioned his scribal work to be greatly sought- after, largely considered, and greatly fought, concurrently. Daniel was prepared by God to stand in the gap for both the nation of Israel and Babylon. Daniels's presence guaranteed the nation's Holy angelic counterpart back-up in the Babylonian Empire. His physical and psychological capacities had been upgraded by God with what appears to be a glimpse of the depth of revelation knowledge that is mind boggling and breathe taking. He was consistently tried and purified while in his service to the nation. God trusted Daniel with visions of the end time,

anointed his hands to record the future of humanity, gave him the capacity to see it, carry it and seal it. What an assignment!

Under Orders

Daniels's food consumption had a heavenly court order on it. Daniels's
diet was to him what Samson's hair care orders were to him. His discipline concerning his eating habits were non-negotiable. Keep in
mind that Babylon probably wasn't hosting kosher foods for their captives. Daniel could not eat the meat of that kingdom and keep his right
standing before the Lord appropriate for his assignment. He understood the value and importance of obedience to His commands and the
consequences of disobedience were apparent as he was living in exile
due to the chosen nation's disobedience. The militaristic prophets are
usually given strict orders from the Lord concerning their dietary habits, health, finances, relationships, what they watch, read, and listen to.
This is because their grooming is different. They must adhere to His
council no matter how minute the instruction may be. They are called
to carry a weighty mantle and anointing and the orders they have been
given can and must be carried out regardless of their unusual situations
and circumstances. In other words, they have no excuse. Their resilience is needed in this hour like never before. They will not fulfill their
purpose without it. Prepare your mind and heart. You will need to be
stretched past your current level of the fear of disappointment on the
road to fulfill your destiny continuously. Embrace your upgrade. You
cannot procrastinate any longer. Your calling is unusual and your
stewardship is held at a higher standard. This is not meant to scare you,

but court-martialing is real. You don't want to birth that reality. The outcome will be catastrophic.

As any other top ranking military official, Daniel was privy to top secret information as his character, conduct, and integrity on earth mirrored his Heavenly clearance. It wasn't his blending in with society that earned him a spot on the honor roll. It was his submission to the God of Israel that propelled him from the spring-board of favor for divine purpose. His heart to carry out a direct order in the midst of chaos and confusion was greatly rewarded. It was his heart to stay faithful amongst so many other gods who were ruling in the damned nation. In what area of your life do you need to come up higher? What are you waiting for? Daniels militaristic-scribal warfare assignment would showcase the end time battle, war strategies, top secrets, and grand-finale outcome of what could be the most misinterpret war in earth's existence.

Daniel 10:12-14 (NJV NIV)

12 Then he continued, "Do not be afraid, Daniel. Since the first day that you set your mind to gain understanding and to humble yourself before your God, your words were heard, and I have come in response to them. 13 But the prince of the Persian kingdom resisted me twenty-one days. Then Michael, one of the chief princes, came to help me, because I was detained there with the king of Persia. 14 Now I have come to explain to you what will happen to your people in the future, for the vision concerns a time yet to come."

The King of Persia's mantle can be recognized through two mediums; national leadership and the demon prince who was assigned to him that came to block Daniels understanding of the revelation. By way of the attack, we can discern that the Persian nation was being used to hinder Israel's progress. Dark forces understood that the revelation that was on its way to Daniel would greatly damage their work and effort. Because you are called to the nations there is a demon prince that is assigned to hinder your mantle just as the prince of Persia was assigned to keep Persia in dominance over Israel. If you are assigned to the nations, your responsibility is to find out from the Holy Spirit what nation(s) you are assigned to. Humility on your part is greatly required as human responsibility will require you to do this as well. Daniels's battle included the nation of Persia which is currently called Iran, and the nation of Greece who took over dominance concerning the nation of Israel after Persia. The chief prince over Israel who is Michael (Israel's Great Prince) came to help Gabriel with the battle. He is also the one who stood up for the Nation of Israel in the time of the vision and is fighting concerning the chosen nation even now.

Daniel 10:12-14 NIV

[12] Then he continued, "Do not be afraid, Daniel. Since the first day that you set your mind to gain understanding and to humble yourself before your God, your words were heard, and I have come in response to them. [13] But the prince of the Persian kingdom resisted me twenty-one days. Then Michael, one of the chief princes, came to help me, because I was detained there with the King of Persia. [14] Now I have come to

explain to you what will happen to your people in the future, for the vision concerns a time yet to come."

Pay attention to your battle, you who are called to the nations. A principality was summonsed to stop the answer to Daniels's prayer. Indeed, this spoke of his authority and rank in the Kingdom as well as in Babylon. You must understand that events that play out on earth, has correlative activity in the spiritual realm. If you are mantled for the nations there is a demon prince that is assigned to hinder your ability as there was with Daniel, as well as, chief prince to counteract your fierce opposition. With all your getting, get understanding. Prophet, you will not perish because of the lack of knowledge. Your movement in the earth activates heaven or hell in your realm of influence. It can also be taken as "an act of war" in the spirit realm. So, move in obedience. May you continue to view Heaven as headquarters and bind and loose according to God-head orders, not the other way around. Heavens court orders are the only ones which are legal, lawful and legislative worthy in the earth realm.

Generational Curses & Territorial Spirits

The Angels we are discussing in this portion of the chapter are what are considered demonic territorial spirits. Fallen Angelic territorial spirits are hostile territorial assassins. Territorial spirits sometimes attach themselves to those who in the natural are positioned in a great place of power. This is because they need to use someone who is in a place of influence in order to access the life and domain of their target. They're highly skilled warrior like entities. If one of these are assigned to your life pay attention. If you do not understand your mantle, authority or the power you walk in, the presence of one of these spirits should make you consider your rank and divine order.

Now, pay close attention to the details of the account I am about to give you as I lay out a clear background of this particular timeline and the many details surrounding these events. For the sake of personally safety and preservation of identity, I'll be changing the names of all those who were involved.

Two and a half years before I surrender to Christ, I was dating a man, let's call him, Jerry. Jerry was friends with a man named Billy for quite some time and he wanted to introduce me to Billy and the rest of his family. Initially, I thought nothing of it, but I couldn't shake the feeling that something was off about Billy and his relatives. They stood out to me, but I was young, naïve, and had no real wisdom concerning spiritual things. As I slowly started to spend more time with them, I noticed that my spirit was not at ease by the invisible activity going on around me. It was only a matter of time before Jerry introduced me to the eldest sister of Billy's family. "The witch" is what ill call her. That was the introduction that changed my life and set me and my family on a path that would have lasting ramifications for over a decade.

Now before I go any further, I want to say that with hindsight being 2020 vision, I am 100% sure that Jerry wasn't aware of what was going on with Billy's family. If anything, I believe he was merely a pawn in the much larger scheme of things. It would behoove us all to remember that our enemies see us long before we see them. I on the other hand could sense that something was off-putting, but again without spiritual wisdom to guide me, I discounted what I was sensing for a very long time.

The Dead Twice and Divine Sentencing

They walk the earth void of light. They are eternally marked by God as the twice dead. Many don't know they exist, but they do. The origin of their spirit man is described in the book of Jude as it describes a parallel of fallen angels leaving their former estate.

Billy's sister was an apostate agent. I always noticed that there was an unusual atmosphere when I was around any member of Billy's family. His sister was the mantle carrier for that bloodline at that time. One of her brothers would always accuse her of being like their grandmother who was a known high-ranking witch. I didn't quite understand these things at the time and I couldn't understand them. It wasn't until a few months after my walk with God had begun that I had been baptized with the Holy Spirit did I begin to understand.

The witch had a notable relationship with the Lord years prior to me meeting their family. I always felt that they were kindred in some kind of way, however I didn't fully understand why I felt that way. I later understood that it was because of the blood covenant of Christ. It had everything to do with the relating blood of Yeshua (Jesus) and nothing to do with the natural bloodline. Her family had concerns for her because she had stopped going to church services and serving the Lord with her life. They had no idea what she had become. Her brothers always had a type of glory resting upon them. I remember saying to her one day that I felt like they were not getting the chance to be them-selves. She answered, "No, no they are not getting to be who they re-ally are". I remember thinking, "Why did she say that so firmly; as if she knew or understood in a different way"? She was operating in apostate witchcraft, which is more subtle and advanced than most craft levels. These are under the rule of high-ranking principalities and ter-ritorial spirits that are assigned to nations and destinies. At that time in my life, I was not redeemed yet and didn't understand most of what I witnessed, until my walk began with Christ and the Holy Spirit taught me pertaining to all I had seen. During those years just before salva-tion, the Lord was showing up in my life in various rescue missions and I always recognize Him. The witch used to tell me stories about how she used to be saved, but "got in trouble". I never understood what she meant by that until later. The Holy Spirit revealed to me that she was what the book of Jude describes as twice dead. Previously she had walked very close to the Lord, but got to a place where she deliberately turned her back on Him. Warriors, you need to understand the severity of the consequences of disobedience. What I learned was that this per-son had gone to the place of no return.

In the old testament, if the Leviticus Priest entered into the Most Holy Place and did so without reverence or proper protocol they would die. The spectators were instructed to place a rope around the priest to pull him out just in case. Sexual immorality was her stronghold. The Lord also revealed to me that she had been court-martialed by the courts of heaven and because to whom much is given, much was required. That last flesh-ride resulted in spiritual death as she had sinned in the spirit after having been given many, many opportunities even years to repent. As well, her office and rank had been taken into account. She knew too much to go back to living in the flesh after living in the spirit in the capacity that she did. *Twice Dead.*

Before this account occurred in my life, I had no idea that such an entity existed. I remember being in her apartment once and seeing her walk down the hall, only to blink, turn around and see her standing directly behind me. I saw many things like this but didn't understand many things at the time. Her assignment was to destroy me before I gave my life to Christ. After sometime, the Lord showed me the opened door to this level of satanic mind control that had opened over my life was facilitated through prayer. One day Billy's sister, wife, and I were having a discussion about unity. Of course, she wanted to "pray" about it. I didn't see what was happening then, but something got my attention towards the end of the prayer. I didn't realize that strategically she was setting things up to lead the prayer. I could hear her use strategic words like "lord, bind us" and so forth. The Lord allowed those words to be highlighted to me even though at the time I didn't know him. It sounded eerie, but that was the first and only time I'd heard her pray so I made light of it. Big mistake. Being taught this way as a child, as she was ending the prayer, I said loudly, "in Jesus' name, amen". From the look on her face, I could tell that she was surprised and that it didn't sit well with her. Sometime before that she told me randomly that my mind was strong. I knew that, so I agreed. What I didn't know was the purpose of that strategic demonic prayer; **to break in**.

*Hebrews 6:*6-8 *NIV*

Therefore, let us move beyond the elementary teachings about Christ and be taken forward to maturity, not laying again the foundation of repentance from acts that lead to death, and of faith in God, [2] instruction about cleansing rites, the laying on of hands, the resurrection of the dead, and eternal judgment. [3] And God permitting, we will do so. [4] It is impossible for those who have once been enlightened, who have tasted the heavenly gift, who have shared in the Holy Spirit, [5] who have tasted the goodness of the word of God and the powers of the coming age [6] and who have fallen away, to be brought back to repentance. To their loss they are crucifying the Son of God all over again and subjecting him to public disgrace. [7] Land that drinks in the rain often falling on it and that produces a crop useful to those for whom it is farmed receives the blessing of God. [8] But land that produces thorns and thistles is worthless and is in danger of being cursed. In the end it will be burned.

She publicly crucified her flesh, was elevated before the people and defiled His temple after being promoted through obedience to realms and dimensions that qualified her for exceedingly *great* authority in the earth. Her sentence would no longer be reversible-exile. She knew too much and went too far. She had a grace to carry out an assignment that would also serve as a witness to her deliberate disobedience as grace is not to be trampled upon; however, it gives you the ability to do what would otherwise be impossible.

Jude 1:1-25 NIV

[1] Jude, a servant of Jesus Christ and a brother of James, to those who have been called, who are loved in God the Father and kept for Jesus Christ:[2] Mercy, peace and love be yours in abundance.[3] Dear friends, although I was very eager to write to you about the salvation we share, I felt compelled to write and urge you to contend for the faith that was once for all entrusted to God's holy people. [4] For certain individuals whose condemnation was written about long ago have secretly slipped in among you. They are ungodly people, who pervert the grace of our God into a license for immorality and deny Jesus Christ our only Sovereign and Lord.

[5] Though you already know all this, I want to remind you that the Lord at one time delivered his people out of Egypt, but later destroyed those who did not believe. [6] And the angels who did not keep their positions of authority but abandoned their proper dwelling—these he has kept in darkness, bound with everlasting chains for judgment on the great Day. [7] In a similar way, Sodom and Gomorrah and the surrounding towns gave themselves up to sexual immorality and perversion. They serve as an example of those who suffer the punishment of eternal fire.

[8] In the very same way, on the strength of their dreams these ungodly people pollute their own bodies, reject authority and heap abuse on celestial beings. [9] But even the archangel Michael, when he was disputing with the devil about the body of Moses, did not himself dare to condemn him for slander but said, "The Lord rebuke you!"[10] Yet these people slander whatever they do not understand, and the very things

they do understand by instinct—as irrational animals do—will destroy them.

[11] Woe to them! They have taken the way of Cain; they have rushed for profit into Balaam's error; they have been destroyed in Korah's rebellion.

[12] These people are blemishes at your love feasts, eating with you without the slightest qualm—shepherds who feed only themselves. They are clouds without rain, blown along by the wind; autumn trees, without fruit and uprooted—twice dead. [13] They are wild waves of the sea, foaming up their shame; wandering stars, for whom blackest darkness has been reserved forever.[14] Enoch, the seventh from Adam, prophesied about them: "See, the Lord is coming with thousands upon thousands of his holy ones [15] to judge everyone, and to convict all of them of all the ungodly acts they have committed in their ungodliness, and of all the defiant words ungodly sinners have spoken against him." [16] These people are grumblers and faultfinders; they follow their own evil desires; they boast about themselves and flatter others for their own advantage.[17] But, dear friends, remember what the apostles of our Lord Jesus Christ foretold. [18] They said to you, "In the last times there will be scoffers who will follow their own ungodly desires." [19] These are the people who divide you, who follow mere natural instincts and do not have the Spirit.

[20] But you, dear friends, by building yourselves up in your most holy faith and praying in the Holy Spirit, [21] keep yourselves in God's love as you wait for the mercy of our Lord Jesus Christ to bring you to

eternal life. [22]Be merciful to those who doubt;[23]save others by snatching them from the fire, to others show mercy, mixed with fear—hating even the clothing stained by corrupted flesh. [24]To him who is able to keep you from stumbling and to present you before his glorious presence without fault and with great joy—[25]to the only God our Savior be glory, majesty, power and authority, through Jesus Christ our Lord, before all ages, now and forevermore! Amen.

On a few occasions, I spent the night at her house after time with her friends and some of her family. One night I briefly woke up and in twilight I witnessed an activity of a blue light that was shooting around the living room like laser beams as I was asleep on the sofa. Then something jumped out of the kitchen window. Her brother was asleep on the floor and simultaneously I heard him say in his sleep "A demon just jumped out of the window".

I learned a lot about access that I'd given this unredeemable witch to my life. After about two months into my walk with God, I was speaking on the phone with my best friend from high school (who has since gone home to the Lord), The phone signaled another call and I clicked over to answer. It was that witch. At that point I didn't have the power to discontinue conversations with her, so I answered. She repeated back to me everything I said on the phone to my friend. That's when I began to understand what was happening and how focused this witch was upon my life. Soon after I was baptized with the Spirit and that witch began to avoid me like the plague. Before that she gave gifts that unbeknownst to me at the time, were meant to gain more power over my life. Things like a lamp with writings on the gift box that if accepted could bring tragedy through the ignorance of agreement. The words on the random gift would start with," "Sister…" I thought it was odd the first time she did it, but again I took it lightly. God protected everyone. I didn't understand it then. The Holy Spirit told me that she received her plans from high-ranking demonic spirits for everyone in her family as well as for me. Turns out, she was assigned to destroy me before I surrendered my life to Christ. God is faithful.

Covenants, Contracts and Agreements

She and 3 of her daughters wore ankle bracelets. I remember the first time I noticed it, it seemed pretty innocent to me. The Lord later told me that it wasn't a mother daughter thing. Those bracelets were place upon those girls because it was her way of keeping at least two people in agreement in the earth with her at all times. Her ultimate assignment was to destroy mantle carriers whose bloodline assignment would serve in a strategic end-time battle. Militaristic Prophet, your life has been a battle zone because there has been a great fight over your destiny and the destiny of your bloodline. God has a Kingdom plan for your family and you have been in satan's way.

As recently as 2008, I was one my way to a sister in Christ who I had asked to write a bio for me. During that time, the Holy Spirit had just released me from an unconventional congregation overseen by a prophet and his wife who was a seer. Looking back, I understand at greater measure why God released me out of a traditional congregation to fellowship at this particular one. Jehovah Gilbbor provides specialized training for the militaristic prophet. Due to the continued personal and congregational related onslaughts, I learned to fight some pretty elevated battles. God will place you in hostile environments in order to teach you the strategies of the enemy and boy did I learn. Back to the aforementioned sister in Christ. I was on my way to her house to pick up my bio. The Holy Spirit had been teaching me about the militaristic mantle at that time and had led me months prior to go to a store that sold military uniforms and to purchase one. So, I did. Sometimes, while I would teach classes about spiritual warfare, I would wear it. That seemed to be the end of it, until one particular day. The Holy Spirit told me to go to a well-known restaurant and change into the uniform. While that may sound crazy to some, I had gotten in the habit of obeying Him regardless of what it looked like in the natural. This particular command is called a prophetic act. A good example of this was the command for the Israelites to march around Jericho in order to break down the walls. When the order is given to perform a prophetic act, you must carry out the order to enact Heaven on earth. God then mobilizes angelic hosts to defeat a territorial spirit in a targeted area through the voice of His Word.

Well, as I arrived to the sister in Christ house to retrieve my bio, I heard three demonic voices in one calling my name. I immediately turned around to see where that grieving voice was coming from. It was her, sitting in a window located upstairs on the condo property across from the sister in Christ. I had been walking with Christ for about 7 years at that time. As I turned to locate the voice, that high ranking diabolical agent said, "Where have you been?" The witch called my name stating, "I've been looking all over for you". Well prophets, I would love to tell you that I said something scriptural to her, but I didn't. I told her to go to hell. God had shown me that it was her final destination so, when did I lie? I knocked in the door and the sister in Christ answered. As I sat on the lower staircase in her condo, I began telling her about what I mentioned in the class that I was teaching at that time called, *"How to Recognize the Strategies of the Enemy"*. She had been to at least 4 of those classes, so I thought she was well informed. She began to tell me about the occurrences in the neighborhood that was stamped with the witch's unredeemable DNA. She said that this woman would fall asleep in her car and the neighbors would try to wake her up, but to no avail. I informed her that it was because she's slips in and out of her body throughout the day. She also said that in her particular condo building, everyone in the building began to have unusual financial issues and the building was cleared out unexpectedly through evictions. She said that she discerned that this woman had something to do with it, but would appear unsuspecting.

She also said that her marriage was on the rocks and that her husband didn't think he loved her anymore. Boom! It all made sense to me. Billy's sister, who was a witch, was strategically positioned in that particular neighborhood to subdue the territory. As I sat on the sister's staircase discussing what happened and going over some of the things I had taught in class, suddenly I could see what happened in the spirit that I was unable to see at first. It was like I was sitting on the staircase in the natural and I was back outside walking up to the sister's door simultaneously. I saw what appeared to be a man standing across from me but not directly facing me. He had the straightest posture I've ever seen. He was caramel in completion and he had on a black priestly robe with a red strip down the right side. He had a sword in the right side of the shaft. He stared at me as I was walking up to the sisters' door. He HATED me. I saw an assignment in his eyes. He wanted to destroy me, but he couldn't. He just watched me walk by. His eyes were very focused on me as they followed me to her doorsteps. I was able to see what I didn't see naturally as I was speaking to her.

When militaristic prophets have been called to certain battles, their angelic counterpart shows up to mark the territory in question. Notice that the Word records that the angel *in the likeness of a man* was standing in front of Joshua. As a counterpart. A holy militaristic angel had marked the ground for battle. When the military of Heaven shows up, this means victory. They come to sanctify the ground. They mark the territory for battle and victory. They represent and defend the pursuit to hegemonize the Kingdom of Heaven.

Joshua 5:13-15

13 Now when Joshua was near Jericho, he looked up and saw a man standing in front of him with a drawn sword in his hand. Joshua went up to him and asked, "Are you for us or for our enemies?" 14 "Neither," he replied, "but as commander of the army of the Lord I have now come." Then Joshua fell facedown to the ground in reverence, and asked him, "What message does my Lord[e] have for his servant?" 15 The commander of the Lord's army replied, "Take off your sandals, for the place where you are standing is holy." And Joshua did so.

During the same time frame, but just before I learned of the witch's location, I was led to move to a house that was located just outside of a closed military base in a brand-new neighborhood. At that time, I didn't have the money or income to live there. I was just moving in unconventional obedience. I lived there for one year. It was a time of one of the most prolific mantle trainings I have had up to date. At least it seems that way. It was in that place I contended with a very strong demon principality. It made all of the sense in the world considering my lifelong spiritual warfare battles in every area of my life. After all, that was the year God taught me concerning the militaristic prophet's classification and I was living on what was once considered military territory.

I was expecting a piece of important mail during a particular week. When it didn't show up, I got concerned. It didn't make sense. I contacted the office of the sender, but they didn't have any meaningful information out side of the fact that it had been mailed off. They advised me to contact the post office, so I did. The post office advised me to contact the Postmaster General. That really stood out to me. Before I contacted the Postmaster General, I was led to do some research. Wow, was I in for a surprise. That was the first I'd heard that name used. A Postmaster General is the chief executive officer of the postal service. This spoke volumes to me. This meant that I was dealing with a principality concerning messages and so forth that was contending for my faith and destiny. Then the Holy Spirit began to speak more to me concerning territorial spirits. Remember, the account I'm giving you took place during the same timeline that I was living in the new ex-military base neighborhood as well as assigned to *another* new congregation. I understood later that this assignment for the sole purpose of anointing and confirming the current residing pastor into the office of the Apostle, wasn't all that was going on. The congregation was under attack as it was in the same neighborhood as the sister in Christ who was helping me with my bio lived in.

Witchcraft Attacks and Relief

A POW may be in captivity due to disobedience to a direct order, which is due to excessive pride, ego and stubbornness; which all constitute under the practice of witchcraft. When God has spoken a word of instruction to someone it is considered by Heaven and should be considered by the heart of the hearer as **a direct order**. Be aware that it will be treated as such. Other reasons may include spiritual and natural imprisonments through generational curses, and indirect consequences due to improper alignment. The rod of correction for such offenses is beyond unbearable. However, it is the grace and mercy of God that gives the ability to survive such a severe consequential experience. There are several references in the Bible concerning such burdens. Jonah was spoken to by the mouth of the Lord and given a command to go to Nineveh to speak to a people whose sin was being acknowledged and had qualified for judgment. God in His Justice cannot legally destroy a nation or individuals without properly informing them of their sin and pending destruction. Jonah served his sentence for disobedience in the belly of a great whale for 3 days - Jonah 1:17. This was revisable exile. That particular witch I mentioned above sentence was eternal. While we understand that God gives us the grace to abound unto every good work, grace also gives us the ability to obey God regardless of the challenges that pertains to the assignment. The militaristic prophet is one who if not early on exposed to the dramatic experience of court martial, will sooner or later gain great comprehensive insight concerning the severity that of the consequence. Divine court martialing is real and it is expedient that this classification understands the requirements to avoid such a dreadful, yet justified verdict.

Satanic Concentration

Satanic concentration is defined as extreme satanic surveillance toward a top Kingdom government official with the intent to alter, interfere, and destroy its intended target. Militaristic prophets are given classified spiritual intelligence that serves to demolish the temporarily rule of territorial spirits as well as the grace to carry out and fulfill assignments that serve as a blueprint and grants unhindered access into naturally concealed spiritual territories, realms and dimensions. Demonic spiritual principalities, also known as territorial spirits are assigned to individuals, cities, nation's neighborhoods, counties, countries, business, bloodlines and etc. Certain individuals are often targeted because they are tied to cities, states, and countries. They may belong to bloodlines with a heavenly mandate to bring forth change either directly or indirectly in that particular generation. Example, a set of parents or a single parent may be tasked with the sole responsibility of raising a child or children who will one day be assigned to a particular city, state, town, nation etc. They would be mantled and assigned the responsibility to execute a Kingdom mandate to change laws, seed the prophetic word in intercession, or shift the mindset of the day. The parents or parent may experience relentless demonically inspired assaults, backlash, extreme hardships, and temptations that will indirectly affect the upbringing of the child. Without proper information and training on the part of the parent(s), this assignment may be hindered by misdirection, thievery, and excessive warfare concerning that child. This warfare can bring great disappointment to those who are intertwined with the destiny of the individual. This type battle can be extreme.

Daniel found himself in a spiritual battle for revelation knowledge that would serve the Church throughout her development on earth and into eternity. He was given a dream/vision and desired to gain understanding concerning it. Little did he know the war that was going on in the stratosphere concerning reception was a battle for the nations. This was a reception that was greatly feared by dark forces. They knew who Daniel was and understood the damage that would be done to the kingdom of darkness if his prayer were ever answered. I understand by revelation knowledge, that the fight was designed to hinder the answer from reaching Daniel with the end in mind that he would collapse in his fasting stance before receiving the revelation of the vision. Daniel's earthly battle during that timeline was just as vicious as the celestial fight. As with the understanding of the vision, came with a responsibility to steward his life under a heavier weight of glory through knowledge. Daniel saw what many of us are seeing today: unprecedented awakening, wars, and battles amongst the nations and more. God used the 21 days of battle to create the capacity to carry the weight of the revelation and deliver it under the scribal anointing and to seal these official kingdom documents it as was instructed.

Keep in mind the book of Daniel was removed from the volume of the book until about 400 years ago.

That's one heck of a fight!!

Territorial battles are relentless. Principalities gain power over a given territory through the sins of the people. They are usually empowered through a witch or warlock in the region. These witches and warlocks are sometimes by birth prophets and apostles gone haywire. Meaning, they don't serve God, however gifts and calling are irrevocable. This is how a strongholds are able to stay in place for generations.

The difference between a witch and a warlock is not related to sex or gender roles.

These two titles have more to do with rank than the gender of the officer. The sacrifice concerning the calling of the militaristic prophet is great, but so is the grace to abound unto every good work. Daniel, Esther, Deborah, Joshua, and Moses are all great examples of the extreme battles that God uses to transform His choice warriors into absolute powerhouses. He put them on heavens honor roll through their obedience by echoing their names and assignments throughout eternity. Throughout the campaigns described in the Book of Joshua, God intervenes by giving Joshua specific instructions regarding the conduct of coming battles, and provided plans for the campaign. God also performed miracles to assist the Israelites in battle and confounded their enemies, including commanding Joshua to stop the motion of the sun from moving across the sky. The days are upon us when these miracles of that caliber will be the new normal.

Another Biblical description of satanic concentration can be seen in the life of Queen Esther. The story of Esther is often expounded upon concerning a queen who was favored by a king and so saved her nation. But the story of Esther is also a historical document that records a massive militaristic operation set in motion by God, continued in default by an enemy of her bloodline and ended by the humility of a God-made Queen. Five centuries had passed since the court-martialing of disgraced, rebel-king Saul. His disobedience kept in motion the bloodline assassins who were now in Queen Esther's timeline and scheduled for execution by the authority of Heavens courts. Saul's submission to high treason through deliberate disobedience was a guarantee that a spirit would be reassigned to a descendent at a later date to extinguish the chosen nation-Israel. Like many of you, Queen Esther was facing the annihilation of her people through of an enemy of her bloodline. You must understand that many of your battles are tied to your bloodline. The sacrifice of her very own life was called to the table to stand in the gap with the knowledge of certain execution and annihilation of her father's house and entire bloodline if her obedience to her purpose was not put in motion in a timely manner. Militaristic prophets, you must understand that your assignments are rare. When there is an impending war on the horizon of your jurisdiction, proper protocol will position you to overcome and reveal the inheritance of victory that will ring throughout history. Esther understood the importance of fasting. Fasting upgraded her favor status in the realm of the spirit and it demanded that the heart of the king would be turned toward the will of the God of Israel.

So now we have this question. Was Queen Esther a mantled militaristic prophet or a wartime prophet?

Well let's take a look at natural and spiritual evidence.

In the natural realm the head of a country also serves as the commander and chief of its military. King Ahasuerus expressed the measure of Esther's grace, favor, and importance his life and kingdom through extending half of his kingdom to her at the sight of her. This measure of favor was meticulously formulated for her purpose and rested upon her life for the sake of her purpose to save a destined nation.

Keep in mind what her cousin Mordecai said;

Esther 4:13-14 NIV

13"Do not think that because you are in the king's house you alone of all the Jews will escape." **14** For if you remain silent at this time, relief and deliverance for the Jews will arise from another place, but you and your father's family will perish. And who knows but that you have come to your royal position for such a time as this?"

Unaware to Esther, God would position her as Queen to obtain the authority in the natural realm, as well as the spirit realm to lead and empower the Hebrew nation to defend themselves against an opposing army of the enemy of her bloodline. Saul's disobedience enabled the reigning territorial spirit that worked through Haman to walk across the bloodline to finish the hit job assigned to the Hebrew people. God always uses a prophet to intersect one chapter in history to another. This is one of the many duties of the office. Sounds pretty militaristic to me. For example, He used John the Baptist to converge the old and new covenant as John was positioned as the threshold that intersected the Door by natural and spiritual bloodline. An example of the work of a territorial spirit in the life John the Baptist is seen through Herod.

We are able to gain a glimpse of John's mantle by the measure of his jurisdictional rule. He was as well, a militaristic prophet created for a certain time in history that would forever tell the story of the friend of the bride grooms' capacity to hear and prepare the way to the Bridegroom.

John 3:28-30

You yourselves can testify that I said, 'I am not the Messiah but am sent ahead of him.' The bride belongs to the bridegroom. The friend who attends the bridegroom waits and listens for him, and is full of joy when he hears the bridegroom's voice. That joy is mine, and it is now complete. He must become greater; I must become less."

He would be sent into a certain spiritual territory in a timeline of sure transition in order to introduce and reinforce the presence of the Kingdom of God in the earth. His testimony would echo throughout eternity of how God became man and stepped into time at the appointed time to rescue, redeem, restore, and reveal the Sons of the Most High God. His shifting in assignment as it pertain to decreasing as the Lamb of God increased, was a mirror of Christ's intercession towards man. Christ decreased to the format of a man in order to increase Himself within us. Mantled for sacrifice and convergence, he served as a legal bridge between God and man who came in the person of Christ. This forerunner: John the Baptist, as they called him was also blood related to Christ. This is an example of how Gods plans for our lives can sometimes include those related to us in the natural realm, not only in the spirit. God has a destiny plan for every family. This is also true concerning mandated marriages. God has a plan. A blueprint.

Called to Marriage

If you are a prophet or an apostle you cannot just marry anyone. God has chosen your mate. He decided Mary and Joseph's union, as it was mandated by heaven according to His purpose. These types of marriages are mandated and militaristic in nature. They serve frontline, destiny, and purpose as prophets and apostles would not be allowed to "choose" their mate.

Disobedience concerning this matter will always end in disaster and summons court-martial, as the mandate usually calls for militaristic classification for the sake of power and authority for an impenetrable assignment. Apostles and Prophets who chooses their mate are sentenced by heaven's courts for doing so. As they do, they open their lives to be ruled by a territorial host. This is where they will eventually come to a place of submission due to the severe distress and gain the wisdom that is required to walk victoriously upon the high hills of the earth. These types of entanglements can take years even a decade or longer to break free from. These territorial spirits are more cunning, as they are strategically assigned to the mantled foundation of the Church as they attach themselves to kings to gain access to the nations. This level of dark monitoring is imposed upon the mantle classification in the same way a nation would monitor its potential opposition. This includes spying and documentation. As I scribe this official document, there is presently a move of God in the earth in relation to revealing the nations and an assertion of the alignment of His bride. This is in relation to an epic transition. We are officially in the timeline of the "end of the hour." Submission in relation to your obedience will take down kingly demonic territorial spirits. Some have been walking through your bloodline from generation to generation, since the fall of Adam. You are about to cross over into a land of inheritance pre-planned and written with the finger of God in the books of destiny and purpose concerning your life and bloodline since before the foundations of the world. You will inadvertently release ordained allotment to others in your line and amongst the nations as well. This is why certain grounds have been fought so hard by demonic forces. Your agreement with God will destroy generational curses hidden under the guise of religion, happenstance, bad decisions, and even Christianity. The workings of word curses, witchcraft, and sabotage made long ago through the flesh by way of blood relation, unbeknownst, is scheduled for annihilation by repentance, and the occupation of Gods Spirit, rule and reign through submission on your part. You can tell when Satan loses his grip off of certain individuals... he gets desperate...still defeated but desperate. Stay focused. The operation and significance of your mantle is not only connected to your bloodline's deliverance, inheritance, and legacy, it's been so brutal, so unusual, so excessive; because there are nations attached to your very breath. You are the mantle carrier for that branch in your bloodline. You've been given the honor to handle great responsibility as John was given the honor to care for the mother of the messiah upon His ordered departure from the earth. Lean in and stay close to His heart. Your heart has been capacitated to beat in alignment with His perfect Will for your bloodline and this generation.

Encroached Ground

The general definition of encroached ground is considered as trespassing on the property, realm or rights of another. Territorial spirits are assigned specifically to do just that. Many believers today are burdened spiritually, as well as naturally because they've allowed themselves to be encroached legally through an assigned, extremely powerful human agent under the influence of a territorial spirit. What make this human host so powerful in their collusion concerning this demon prince-territorial spirit is solely their will and commitment to the workings of their flesh. I was divinely assigned to a Pastor who presided over a local assembly of believers. The Holy Spirit told me that this particular Pastor was being summoned by the Lord to step into the fivefold ministry of an Apostle. This Pastor had served the people and the community for over 20 years and had been released to serve faithfully from a well-known Christian organization. Upon going to this particular assembly, I had the opportunity to speak with the Pastor concerning what the Spirit of the Lord had spoken to me. He confirmed the words that were given to me and I attended the church for about 2-3 months. I could see that there was great warfare in the Church in connection to the leaders. I set up an appointment again to speak with the pastor about the activation concerning the promotion in question. It was then that I began to see the open door to all of the excessive warfare that was holding back the congregation. The warfare that was a direct result of the pride and arrogance flowing through the assembly from the pastor kept the pastor bound to the ground. I say this because upon one of my last visits to the assembly I saw in the spirit; a demonic force holding down the shoulders of the pastor. Needless to say, the mindset-stronghold on this assembly was great. The pastor hosted weekly services on a local television channel and was overly concerned with his audience. This pastor missed his time of visitation because of pride. I was released by God from the assignment. When assigned to encroached ground, we must be open to receive specific instructions from the Lord before we move forward to possess the land. Moving without clear direction, wisdom and understanding, serves to thwart the mission. He is a God of order.

Chapter 4 Review:

1) **What does your spiritual inheritance usually include and why?**

   Your spiritual inheritance usually includes the convergence two different bloodlines to bring forth. It is a spiritual inheritance.

   Meaning it flows directly from the mind of Christ- the heart of Gods plan with the intent to bless and fulfill His plan for humanity.

2) **What is satanic concentration?**

   Satanic concentration is defined as extreme satanic surveillance toward a top Kingdom government official with the intent to alter, interfere and destroy its intended target- Teresa Martin.

3) What does strict orders look like for the militaristic prophets and why so strict?

The Militaristic Prophets is usually given strict orders from the Lord concerning their dietary habits (a very big deal) health, finances, and relationships, what you watch, read, listen to. This is because your grooming is different. You must adhere to His council no matter how minute the instruction may be. You are called to carry a weighty mantle and anointing and the orders you have been given can and must be carried out regardless of your unusual situations and circumstances. In other words, you have no excuse.

4) What are territorial spirits?

Fallen Angelic territorial spirits are hostile territorial assassins. Territorial spirits attach themselves to those who, in the natural-are positioned in a great place of power

They come with an assignment to assassinate their target. They're highly skilled warrior like entities.

If one of these are assigned to your life; pay attention.

If you do not understand your mantle, authority or the power you walk in, the presence of one of these should make you consider your rank and divine order.

Chapter Four Summary:

From strict order, to intense battles with territorial spirits the militaristic prophet's mantle is protected and respected in various arenas of life. They witness epic celestial battles as well as lead them within the realm of the earth. They contend with demonic generational agents and the dead twice alike. They are positioned in thresholds of society in order to bring forth reformation and Kingdom mandates.

Strategic Prayer:

May every work of darkness in my realm of influence be exposed and dismantled by the council of the Godhead. Let every strategic demonic assignment be brought to an instant halt as you advance the Kingdom of your dear son within the hearts of your chosen. I thank you for divine protection as it granted by the will of God for my life, legacy and bloodline. I decree that the ruling spirit in my life and those I am assigned to is the Holy Spirit and no weapon formed against your people will prosper.

CHAPTER FIVE

The Wartime Prophet

~~~~~

*Our mental warfare is allowed to Militarize the
mind against satanic intrusions.*
~Teresa Martin

Scripture Reference: Jeremiah 1:6-8NIV

6 "Alas, Sovereign LORD," I said, "I do not know how to speak; I am
too young." **7** But the LORD said to me, "Do not say, 'I am too young.'
You must go to everyone I send you to and say whatever I command
you. **8** Do not be afraid of them, for I am with you and will rescue you,"
declares the LORD.

What is the difference between Wartime Prophets and Militaristic Prophets?

Wartime prophets are stealth warriors who's mantle function serves
the ability to negotiate on the national level, (in the realm of the spirit

as well as the natural realm), serve their generation and mantle assignment as a reformer, advocate for justice, as well as the ability to nurture their assigned subjects through war, and rumors of war. They are war-scribal historians and are usually transitional prophets. They are destiny carriers who are specifically and strategically deposited into the earth for a specific assignment that has been delegated to a certain generation.

These assignments may include turning points in history such as a nations transition into power, correction and exile, an impending war of annihilation, national leadership, including civil rights movements and events similar in nature. They are often overlooked as wartime prophets because of their peculiar, various expressions. They can be identified in scripture through research and diligent study. However, a militaristic prophet is *easily* recognized in scripture, as they mainly and fluently function as a commander such as Moses, Joshua, Deborah, Saul, and David who all ruled by leading Israel's military during the times of war. The obvious. The militaristic prophet and the wartime prophet's mantle are in likeness, but differ in rank. An idea of what this looks like would be similar to how all prophets are seers but not all seers are prophets. Another example of this would be how all prophets are intercessor but not all intercessor are prophets. Equivalent to how an apostle as a 5-fold officer can function at any time as a prophet or one of the other 3 offices. However, a prophet who is promoted as an apostle has a different measure of grace upon their lives. They operate differently. What makes a prophet so authentic is their spirit. A prophet's spirit is like no other. The prophet's peculiar spiritual make-up does not cease to function amid excessive trials and testing. Neither does an apostle have a prophet's spirit in that context, however, the spirit-man of the prophet rests upon the apostle to function in office and mantle likewise. So, when we speak of others such as Jeremiah, Nehemiah, Isaiah, and Esther the difference in expression is apparent. This because they were not militaristic prophets as it traditionally pertains to a commander or an influential exceptional leader. They were war-time prophets. This is what I call a similar difference. Jeremiah was a wartime prophet who was solely tasked with the responsibility of warning Israel of the judgment of exile. His mantle included the function of the intercessor, scribal historian, an artist of poetry, social reformer, and national leader (amongst his people). He was also a strategist.

This prophet mentioned repentance more times than any other first covenant prophet. He was considered a major prophet in history recorded in the Bible because of his ministry assignments and the impact it served. These titles (major and minor) are given based upon prophetic performance in a turning point in time as well as the density of the given assignment(s). Major transitions identify innovative solutions and assignments i.e., apostles and prophets. Jeremiah was positioned at a certain time in history that allows us to take a glimpse into Israel's journey through exile by way of his writings. Throughout Jeremiah's life, we are comforted by his "confessions" recorded in scripture concerning his feelings towards God as they revealed a very human side of this major prophet's mindset; even his heart.

Jeremiah 11:18-23; 12:1-6, 15:10-21; 17:14-18; 18:19-23 and 20:7-13 NIV

A wise and passionate reformer- he encouraged social justice and peace concerning his people. It would make sense that the treatment of an exiled nation in the land of its captivity would be harsh and deceptive. Jeremiah fought for social justice, relief for his people, and continued to oppose those who wanted to fight their way out of their new location. He encouraged Israel to get use to the new place as their sentence wouldn't be lifted any time soon. While in exile, he served as a type of prophetic governor of Israel while in exile in that he would oversee the care, conduct, and overall wellbeing of the nation.

Jeremiah 22:1-2 NIV

This is what the LORD says: Do what is just and right. Rescue from the hand of the oppressor the one who has been robbed. Do no wrong or violence to the foreigner, the fatherless or the widow, and do not shed innocent blood in this place. This is what the LORD says: "Go down to the palace of the king of Judah and proclaim this message there...

Daniel the Wartime Prophet

Entrusted with unique end-time vision of catastrophic events, unprecedented leadership, epic visits from Angels, and presented with opportunities and trials that would run the average human batty; Daniel was a wartime prophet who was exiled to Babylon at approximately the

age of 17. The sovereignty of God positioned him in a very high position in Babylon. A wartime prophet is graced with the vision and
knowledge of future events, while being burden by continuous death
threats and the hardship of their assignment. One must have the keys
to unlock destiny through maturity. This comes through years of re-
finement. God led Daniel's friends into the fire in order to prepare
them for the next place of promotion, stewardship and rule. It will be
no different for you. Israel was once again in exile due to disobedience.
Daniel like Queen Esther was positioned in the political realm as an
act of mercy towards the children of Israel while in exile. The Hebrew
nation was once again facing potential annihilation from a group of
haters who sought to kill Daniel because an excellent spirit was in him
as well as he did not participate in Babylon's traditional lifestyle and
worship ceremonies. The term exile is basically defined as a time when
your territory has been stripped from your rule. When God shows up
in mercy to return it to you, a bow is in order to the King.

Esther

A War-time prophet who was positioned to save a nation, laced with
the grace of God, Esther was thrust upon the scene as a potential Queen
who would later serve to stand in the gap for her native country-men
at a time of the premeditated genocide of the ancient Hebrew people.
Her training and development included a good dose of loss, pain, lone-
liness, and emptiness. We gain this perspective through scripture as
we learn of the loss of both her parents at an early age, and the over-

seeing of her cousin Mordecai. Historical documents records there being a time when the king- ungraciously orders every virgin in the region to be brought to his kingdom to select a new queen.

Proverbs 21:1 NIV

The king's heart is like a stream of water directed by the LORD; he guides it wherever he pleases.

Now that we've gained a background into the life of this chosen queen, let's take a look at the queen's mantle. Queen Esther's mantle included the function of a national leader as a political official and intercessor. She was graced with a beauty, coupled with favor that served to realign protocol in the very powerful and influential nation of Persia. She was a wartime prophet who was equipped with access into the heart of a king as it gave her his ear and the power to influence his decisions. She had been in preparation for this assignment of intercession from conception. She possessed the grace that is needed in the hard place.

Serving Time

Time is a consequence to disobedience. It is a measurement use to bring discipline, proper alignment and order to the 3 part being of mankind. We are not supposed to serve time. Time serves us. We must stop giving it authority over us by stating that we "don't have time for", whatever. Time is an element, a prophetic fire and a witness to what you did when it was assigned to the earth through man's deliberate disobedience. Time will tell it, is not just a random phrase although most "random phrases" have some truth to it. Time is an elder. Iniquity gives it access to rule over us. When we repent, we are granted access to the knowledge concerning its service to us. God uses it as a cell guard when crime is presented. The fall of man was criminal to say the least. This is one of the reasons why when we are in a prophetic atmosphere or environment time seems to disappear. Even when we are spending quality time with the Lord in prayer, study, etc. time seems to disappear. Its authority is limited where righteousness rules. The concept of time also falls as well in the category of an instrument. This specific instrument was created and is used to monitor, and produce purpose in a supernatural sequenced manner. After time as we know it finishes its current assignment, it will be reassigned and possibly renamed for a greater purpose. Wow, time will, after a while, receive its promotion and reward for serving man- the Descendants of YHWH Elohim. What an assignment!

Purpose exists in the heart of man and nothing truly productive happens in this realm if it doesn't include the assistance of a human being. God speaks of restoring the years in Joel 2:25. The idea that years can be restored is not something we necessary believe. We've yet to see certain promises from God; however, this is the timeline in the revelation of the One New Man that we have moved into the fullness of time. Years were stolen and years will be restored.

Joel 2:25

I will restore the years the locus, the cankerworm and the palmer worm has eaten.

Chapter 5 Review:

1) **What is the difference between a wartime prophet and a militaristic Prophet?**

The militaristic prophet and the wartime prophet's mantle are in likeness, but differ in rank. An idea of what this looks like would be similar to how all prophets are seers but not all seers are prophets. Another example of this would be how all prophets are intercessor but not all intercessor are prophets.

2) **What is the role and purpose of the wartime prophet?**

They are war- scribal historians, transitional prophets whose assignments include, a nations transition into power (which are turning points in history), correction and exile, an impending war of annihilation, national leadership, including civil rights movements and the like. They are often overlooked as wartime prophets because of their peculiar, various expressions.

3) **What does some of wartime's Prophet's responsibilities include?**

Some can be solely tasked with the responsibility of warning a nation of the judgment, the function of the intercessor, scribal historian, an artist of poetry, social reformer and national leader and more.

4) What was Queen Esther's wartime mantle function including?

Queen Esther's mantle included the function of a national leader as a political official and intercessor. She was graced with a beauty-coupled with favor that served to realign protocol in the very powerful and influential nation of Persia.

She was a wartime prophet who was equipped with access into the heart of a king as it gave her his ear and the power to influence his decisions. She had been prepared for this moment of intercession since conception. She possessed the grace that is needed in the hard place.

Chapter Five Summary:

The wartime prophet is created, groomed and dedicated by God to their assignment. They are empowered and position, educated in various wartime events and timelines in history as well as the present. They have the ability to articulate Gods precise instruction, will, purpose and destiny in any environment, to any people and nation. The differ from the militaristic prophetically only in in rank and they serve their generation and mantle assignment as a reformer, advocate for justice, as well as the ability to nurture their assigned subjects through war, rumors of war, transitions of power. They are war-scribal historians and are usually a transitional prophet. Militaristic prophets usually function as both.

Prayer Strategy:

The Anointing to build is upon my life I as I advance the Kingdom of God through submission to your perfect will. Thank you for the ability to manifest your blueprint in times of war and chaos. Grant me acceleration and necessary provision that will cause me to fulfill your necessary requirements during times of spiritual war, building and rebuilding. You are the greatest architect-a master builder. Thank you for stretching my faith as I submit to your perfect will. So be it!!

CHAPTER SIX

The Agent of Reformation

✧✦✧✦✧

Reformers stand before kings and commoners alike. They serve divinely with a heart for the people, purpose, and progress.
~Teresa Martin

Scripture Reference: Isaiah 40:3

The voice of him that crieth in the wilderness, prepare ye the way of the LORD, make straight in the desert a highway for our God.

A Reformer is someone who is called to bring about change in an existing system. They are mentally, emotionally, and spiritually wired as change agents. They are positioned in turning points in history to bring about a shift in sectors of society through business, art, marriage, religion, bloodlines, and nations. They are strategically deposited in key times in history to accomplish the most daunting task. They are passionate social reformers who bring light to injustices and revolution to the status quo. Reformers are relentless in their pursuit of their passion. They are hardwired to Heaven, an instrument of sight and sound, a force to be reckoned with. They are fierce leaders, professional, and abstract instruments. They are graced with an apostolic anointing to build and rebuild. They carry an uncanny anointing to see as well. Reformers stand before kings and commoners alike. They serve divinely with a heart for the people, purpose, and progress. In this time of reformation, an emergence is coming about. It is expedient that you are educated concerning you gift and calling. The reformer is clothed with courage and often carries a dual, sometimes multi-mantles. This means most militaristic prophets couple as reformers. Here are some general characteristics of a reformer:

Characteristics of A Reformer

1) Courageous

2) Passionate

3) Determined

4) Visionary

5) Historian

6) Builder/rebuilder

7) Scribal

8) Detail Oriented

9) Tenacious

10) Insightful

11) Resilient

The fire that burns in the bones of this engineer of social reformation is produced by the absolute passion that burns within. Reformers are wired with a level of determination that treads down everything that opposes the path of the vision. They are quick learners with the vision and details for the assignment that raises eyebrows as it confronts the counterfeit reality and dismantles the masterminds behind the previous invention. Empowered with a photographic memory, this agent is top gun and hard to trick. They are detail oriented and love alignment and order. When operating in their element they are fierce contenders, tenacious in battle, and thrive at problem solving. They are usually described as what people call empaths and introverts, as they may be loners. They may also have scribal tendencies. These are the ones who God has raised up to interrupt the status quo. God is not sending those who are self-preserving concerning their comfort at the expense of true destiny and legacy. He has chosen those who will choose Him. He is harvesting His children from amongst the nations and there will be no more compromise or contamination concerning His Vessels of Honor. Reformers are built to last. They are certified change agents who carry a weight of vision that shifts the influence of mountain mandates, which shift the mentality of culture on earth. This agent is strategically sent as they carry the winds of change that brings forth reformation. Reformers are history makers, who carry a fire in their bones that defies death until the mission is complete. They are resilient warriors who will stop at nothing to accomplish what has been purposed within them. The works of their hands echoes throughout history and sets the standards from the farming fields to the nations of the world. They are often used as a sickle in the hands of the Lord of the harvest. They are deliverers, freedom-fighters, law-maker, artist, janitors, etc. They don't just make a perforation in the fabric of history. These ground-breaking change agents challenge societal norms and serves to indent a new reality into to scrolls of history; changing the game and the players who participate. They change history and unlock dimensions of the blueprint most intelligently. Move stealthily as you keep this in mind. Keep your vision close as you manifest the blueprint. Reformation runs concurrent with recovery. Reformation is a master in social value as it relates to the idea of recreating and manifesting.

To recover generally means to return to the original intent. They are partners as it relates to accomplishing the task at hand. Reformation aligns and brings order a given situation. It is considered an upgrade in origin in terms of its assignment. The militaristic prophet as an agent of reformation is trained by great affliction. This agent is trained to invade and subdue its intended target.

The anointing provides the power and authority to tear down the strongholds that exist in the minds of the people who are in bondage to the uncorrected, off course reality. These realities exist through the empowerment of systems and protocols. Every system that exists in the earth that does not derive from Kingdom of Heaven is Egyptian and Babylonian in nature. Those words in this context imply slavery and assimilation.

It is the power of agreement that reinforces any reality. Belief strengthens the structure, substance, and optical illusion of every thought. This is why the words of a reformer are extremely weighty and influential. God mantles and trains the reformer to stand in high places. The reformer has clear, undisputed vision of the future. They are infused with the oxygen of the reality of their assignment. They are wired to meet the necessary requirements to fulfill their mandate at any cost.

Psalms 18:33 NIV

He makes my feet like the feet of a deer; he causes me to stand on the heights. He trains my hands for battle; my arms can bend a bow of bronze.

Reformers are a game changer by design. They bring a divine reversal or a shift to the very territories they are assigned to as they are created to carry an anointing of a divine interruption and to restructure systems. The militaristic mantle operates in full display when operating under the functional anointing of a reformer. We are able to see this anointing in full operation in the life of the Messiah-Christ. Yeshua Hamashiach came to the earth not only as our redeemer, but as a reformer as well. Every move He made brought forth reformation. He healed the sick without medicine on the Sabbath, and he raised the Lazarus on the 4th day. He exercised His authority over the weather and climate and single handedly (not outside of the authority of the Father) shut down the entire religious system and death itself.

Mathew 12:1-13 NIV

12 At that time Jesus went through the grain fields on the Sabbath. His disciples were hungry and began to pick some heads of grain and eat them. 2 When the Pharisees saw this, they said to him, "Look! Your disciples are doing what is unlawful on the Sabbath."

3 He answered, "Haven't you read what David did when he and his companions were hungry? 4 He entered the house of God, and he and his companions ate the consecrated bread—which was not lawful for them to do, but only for the priests. 5 Or haven't you read in the Law that the priests on Sabbath duty in the temple desecrate the Sabbath and yet are innocent? 6 I tell you that something greater than the temple is here. 7 If you had known what these words mean, 'I desire mercy, not sacrifice,' you would not have condemned the innocent. 8 For the Son of Man is Lord of the Sabbath."9 Going on from that place, he went into their synagogue, 10 and a man with a shriveled hand were there. Looking for a reason to bring charges against Jesus, they asked him, "Is it lawful to heal on the Sabbath?"11 He said to them, "If any of you has a sheep and it falls into a pit on the Sabbath, will you not take hold of it and lift it out? 12 How much more valuable is a person than a sheep! Therefore, it is lawful to do good on the Sabbath."13 Then he said to the man, "Stretch out your hand." So he stretched it out and it was completely restored, just as sound as the other. 14 But the Pharisees went out and plotted how they might kill Jesus. His overall life and daily assignment revealed the Fathers heart for humanity.

When a militaristic prophet is summons and deployed their entrance into the new as well as their exit out of the old serves to bring reformation. Let's remember, the Lamb was slain before the foundations of the world, however, that eternal act was completely fulfilled when Jesus took the blood of man and put it on the Mercy Seat. That act solidified the God-plan to reform man to his original intent. This made it a militaristic move as was the wile in the garden on the adversary's part. The strategy was to encroach the territory.

Nehemiah the Reformer

The Book of Nehemiah was a reformers wartime journal- inspired by the Holy Spirit. The Prophet Nehemiah was governor of Persian Judea under Artaxerxes I of Persia (465-424 BC). Nehemiah was a wartime prophet who served to bring reformation to the Children of Israel after enduring the trauma of exile. God strategically positioned Nehemiah to serve as Governor of Persian Judea. During his reign Nehemiah re-inforced reformation in the hearts of the people of God. This was a time in history when God would move upon the heart of His servant with such a fierce passion to rebuild in record time, and to completely restore what had been brought to ruins. What about you? What have you been called to rebuild?

Nehemiah outlines the plan to accomplish a God-task without inter-ruption. The grace to accelerate was given to him to lead and succeed through his apostolic mantle to rebuild. Nehemiah endured slander, death threats, and threats to be investigated by the reining government. He was ordered to stop his work immediately by those who were like-wise in some form of authority. They spoke prophetic words to him, concerning him in order to deceive him. There was major conflict and animosity surrounding the rebuilding of the wall. The enemies of his purpose and Israel's destiny served as a continual nuisance to the ap-pointed work. These opposer's feared losing power and influence over the people. They stopped at nothing in their attempts to overthrow the rebuilding. Fear and intimidation creeped in on every side. So, what is your opposition? You must know without a shadow of a doubt that in Christ, you are well able to accomplish the task at hand. You were not created without a plan. God is not a freestyler. He is the greatest architect and He has a blueprint. Heaven knows your location and is on higher alert concerning your every movement. Heaven provides a court reporter that records your every word and every other word that concerns you. You are not unattended.

Matthew 12:36 NIV

But I tell you that everyone will have to give account on the day of judgment for every empty word they have spoken.

Listen, territorial spirits know that your God appointed work will be a threat to their current power and influence. You become an agitation and an assignment to be neutralize in the earth realm. It is important that you don't mistake the identities of those who make themselves available through host. They are appointed mockers. Expect these types of host to carry their fair weight in influence. Opposer's will usually, but not always be the loudest to make themselves known. They can't help it. These hosts often pursue power to ensure dominion in the lives of those they want to control. Nehemiah understood his stature and the depths of his assignments. He had a heart for justice as he was a mantled reformer as well. Grace for restoration rest upon its subject. Courage is an attribute that come relatively easy to this mantle classification. They are wired to problem solve and are fierce negotiators. To be in the presence of this trained, refined, multi-mantled-militaristic feature is to be aware of their posture of excellence, as the glory and the grace of God eludes from the life of the classification.

The Apostolic Mandate

The Apostolic anointing and gifting empower systems. The shifting of a system or, structure in any realm will take an apostolic mandate that is empowered by and apostolic anointing, gifting or mantle. The difference between the three is that an apostolic anointing and gifting gives one the ability to operate in the apostolic at certain given points in time. The apostolic mantle belongs to the office, therefore the ranking and responsibility is greater. The militaristic prophet is dual apostolic reinforcement agent. The death and resurrection of Lazarus details an apostolic move which makes it a militaristic move. This is one of the many reasons why Jesus waited another day and then began to go to the one who He loved who was reported sick. His orders were strict and strategic as He moved in militaristic precision. Notice the voice of doubt is always present when a massive move of God is set in motion. These are usually last-minute deception blows that if understood, serves as an ID badge concerning the nature of the move.

Operation Lazarus

Special operations differ from conventional operations. The resurrection of Lazarus displayed strategic infiltration and a hostile takeover concerning Kingdom assets. Jesus was stealth in His conquest to destroy the mental stronghold that fortified the thinking of the ancient Hebrew people. Ancient literature records that the Hebrew people of that day believed that once a person died, their spirit hovered over the body of the deceased for three days. Then after three days, their spirit would either go to the bosom of Abraham or hell. This mental construct created a systematic way of thinking that blocked some of them from receiving the gift of faith that would offer them redemption. We have evidence of this in scripture.

John 11:28-45 NIV

28 After she had said this, she went back and called her sister Mary aside. "The Teacher is here," she said, "and is asking for you." 29 When Mary heard this, she got up quickly and went to him. 30 Now Jesus had not yet entered the village, but was still at the place where Martha had met him. 31 When the Jews who had been with Mary in the house comforting her, noticed how quickly she got up and went out, they followed her, supposing she was going to the tomb to mourn there.32 When Mary reached the place where Jesus was and saw him, she fell at his feet and said, "Lord, if you had been **here, my brother would not have died."**33 When Jesus saw her weeping, and the Jews who had come along with her also weeping, he was deeply moved in spirit and troubled. 34 "Where have you laid him?" he asked. **"Come and see, Lord," they replied.** 35 Jesus wept. 36 Then the Jews said, "See how he loved him!" 37 But some of them said, "Could not he who opened the eyes of the blind man have kept this man from dying?" 38 Jesus, once more deeply moved, came to the tomb. It was a cave with a stone laid across the entrance. 39 "Take away the stone," he said. "But, Lord," said Martha, the sister of the dead man, "by this, time there is a bad odor, for he has been there four days." 40 Then Jesus said, "Did I not tell you that if you believe, you will see the glory of God?" 41 So they took away the stone. Then Jesus looked up and said, "Father, I

thank you that you have heard me. [42] I knew that you always hear me, but I said this for the benefit of the people standing here, that they may believe that you sent me." [43] When he had said this, Jesus called in a loud voice, "Lazarus, come out!" [44] The dead man came out, his hands and feet wrapped with strips of linen, and a cloth around his face. Jesus said to them, "Take off the grave clothes and let him go."[45] Therefore many of the Jews who had come to visit Mary, and had seen what Jesus did, believed in him."

Take note that it wasn't until after Mary left for the grave site that the audience was in place to witness the decimation of a stronghold created by a series of reinforced beliefs that created one of the strongest mindsets of the day. This mission was a challenge. There was much at stake. The odds were stacked against this breakthrough from the beginning.

John1:11 NIV

A man named Lazarus was sick. He was from Bethany, the village of Mary and her sister Martha. [2] (This Mary, whose brother Lazarus now lay sick, was the same one who poured perfume on the Lord and wiped his feet with her hair.) [3] So the sisters sent word to Jesus, "Lord, the one you love is sick." [4] When he heard this, Jesus said, "This sickness will not end in death. No, it is for God's glory so that God's Son may be glorified through it." [5] Now Jesus loved Martha and her sister and Lazarus. [6] So when he heard that Lazarus was sick, he stayed where he was two more days, [7] and then he said to his disciples, "Let us go back to Judea."[8] "But Rabbi," they said, "a short while ago the Jews there tried to stone you, and yet you are going back? [9] Jesus answered,

"Are there not twelve hours of daylight? Anyone who walks in the daytime will not stumble, for they see by this world's light. ₁₀ It is when a person walks at night that they stumble, for they have no light." ₁₁ After he had said this, he went on to tell them, "Our friend Lazarus has fallen asleep; but I am going there to wake him up." ₁₂ His disciples replied, "Lord, if he sleeps, he will get better." ₁₃ Jesus had been speaking of his death, but his disciples thought he meant natural sleep. ₁₄ So then he told them plainly, "Lazarus is dead, ₁₅ and for your sake I am glad I was not there, so that you may believe. But let us go to him." ₁₆ Then Thomas (also known as Didymus said to the rest of the disciples, "Let us also go, that we may die with him." Jesus chose to stay where He was despite the fact that He "loved" Lazarus.

We know that Jesus loved everyone but emphasis is put on His love relationship with Lazarus. I believe it's safe to say that He had an immediate desire to comfort the sibling family- which is apparent in any love relationship. Nevertheless, He waited at the command of the Father by awaiting the time of departure as well as yielding His/our delegated power over death. Remember, it was the Father who raised Him from the dead. Resurrection and redemption are the Fathers solution to the death and error.

John 5:19 NIV

Jesus gave them this answer: 'Very truly I tell you, the Son can do nothing by himself; he can do only what he sees his Father doing, because whatever the Father does the Son also does.

John 11:4 NIV

When he heard this, Jesus said, "This sickness will not end in death. No, it is for God's glory so that God's Son may be glorified through it." ₅ Now Jesus loved Martha and her sister and Lazarus. ₆ So when he heard that Lazarus was sick; Mary's faith had only been stretched to the extent of the miracles that she witnesses through Jesus." The resurrection of Lazarus after 4 days; increased her faith capacity and brought the Jews to ultimate believe.

John 11:45 NIV

₄₅ Therefore many of the Jews who had come to visit Mary, and had seen what Jesus did believed in him.

The chapter records that He had a special love relationship with Mary and Martha as well. It's important that we pay attention to how hard it had to be in His humanness to witness the pain of death concerning those who were close to His heart. Militaristic prophet, when you are assigned to someone God will not only give you secret details concerning their life and heart, He will allow you to feel what they feel. This is in association with the intercessor within you.

John 11:35 NIV

Jesus wept.

It was after two days from hearing what happened to Lazarus that Jesus notified His disciples that it was time to go back to Judea. The statement raised concerns amongst the chosen because just a short while before that time there was an assassination attempt made upon His life. But Yeshua (Jesus) began to speak using the night and day as a description of His ability to see past the natural realm. So far, there is bad news that has manifested concerning close friends of His who were in distress concerning sickness and the fear of death. Filled with uncertainty they sent word to Christ hoping He would heal their loved one as they had witnessed Jesus do many times before and with ease. He then announces Lazarus' updated condition and His assignment to "wake him up". This was a covert operation. A covert operation is basically defined as a military operation that conceals the sponsor. This type of operation serves to strengthen the mission objective by deliberately hiding the expected end of the operation. This type of operation is used in society more often than not. This type of move is served on a stealth platter. This is one of the reasons why operating in integrity is a must! When you are facing a battle, there has been a hard inquiry of your bloodline. In fact, many of the battles you have and are facing are a result of unrepentant sin in your bloodline. This is one of the reasons why a people, place, or nation can go around the mountain over and over again. Unresolved sin is related to a fixed mindset and a harden heart.

John 11:11 NIV

After he had said this, he went on to tell them, "Our friend Lazarus has fallen asleep; but I am going there to wake him up.

Chapter Six Review:

1. What is a reformer?

A reformer is someone who is called to bring about change in an existing system. They are mentally, emotionally and spiritually wired as change agents. They are positioned in turning points in history to bring about a shift in sectors of society through business, religion, bloodline and nations. They are strategically deposited in key times in history to accomplish the most daunting task. They are passionate social reformers who bring light to injustices and revolution to the status quo. They bring light to darkness and are relentless in their pursuit of their passion. They are hardwired to Heaven- an instrument of sight and sound- a force to be reckoned with. They are fierce leaders, professional and abstract instruments.

2. How do reformers operate?

Reformers are a game changer by design. They bring a divine reversal or a shift to the very territories they are assigned to as they are created to carry an anointing of a divine interruption and to restructure systems. They are history makers, and historians who carry a fire in their bones that defies death until the mission is complete. They are resilient warriors who will stop at nothing to accomplish what has been purposed within them. The works of their hands echoes throughout history and sets the standards from the farming fields to the nations of the world.

3. What is a covert operation?

A covert operation is loosely defined as a military operation that conceals the sponsor. This type of operation serves to strengthen the mission objective by deliberately hiding the expected end of the operation. This type is used in society more often than not. This type of move is served in a stealth platter.

CHAPTER SEVEN

The Emerging Militaristic Prophet

❧

Be certain, no matter how hard and unusual your warfare is,
Satan cannot do to you what he has been wanting to do and if
you stay in God's Will, He will never be able to.
~Teresa Martin

Scripture Reference: Deuteronomy 31:6

Be strong and courageous. Do not be afraid or terrified because of them, for the LORD your God goes with you; he will never leave you nor forsake you."

Witchcraft prayers are designed to change the inner and outer structure of a reality. This gives it a place to dwell in this dispensation of time because there's no place in Heaven for it, and it has no real power outside of operating through a human vessel in the earth. Witchcraft is a spirit. Word curses are sent to release the substance of what is in them: wickedness and error. Think about it. When you go through what I call a "quickly disabled attack", even after apologies and good communication there has still been a change to the structure of the re-lationship. This is why the foundation of every relationship must be Christ. He is a sure foundation. God uses these sudden, meticulously calculated attacks to shift the intended target into a greater position of alignment and power. This is why certain relationships are fought so hard. The convergence of certain relationships would be catastrophic to the plans of dark forces. An authentic (God ordained not fleshly desired) destiny and purpose covenant will always be attacked because of the power it holds in the earth. Certain attacks are designed to utterly destroy instantly, not just use your life for years until you're destroyed. Those attacks feel `stronger and appear to last longer because of the no weapon principle. Herein is the wear down method in effect. Be certain, no matter how hard and unusual your warfare is, Satan cannot do to you what he has been wanting to do and if you stay in God's Will, he will never be able to. That is not to say that you won't have fierce battles, but his ultimate intent will not be accomplished. Total alignment brings fulfillment of purpose. God causes every attack to work together for your good. In this, God is glorified, Christ is preached and Holy Spirit is obeyed.

It's hard to receive healing when modern Christianity has a fundamen-tal frame work of pretending not to be 'moved" in the midst of battle. There's an attitude of "strength" that is on optical steroids that gives the insinuation that if you are going through a battle or trial of any kind then something must be wrong. Something is definitely off about this. This off kilter mindset makes healing practically impossible in many cases. Psychological warfare is no joke. Excessive battles without re-lent are traumatic. Yeshua (Jesus) was a man of sorrows; aquatinted with grief, yet somehow, we've excluded that as part of the salvation benefit package. We forget that the process is a process. However, we have a healer. He desires to make us one again- spirit, soul and body.

In ancient scripture our great King consistently revealed His oneness as the God of Israel. One day the Lord said to me, "You are one". He then began to give me understand concerning how He created us. We are spirit, soul and body. Human Beings have a three part existence. One cannot fully function without the other. During the fall, by coming under the subjection of the voice of a fallen angel, mankind was separated from within. This is where chaos and confusion came in-through us. We were created to live in inner harmony with our selves. When we don't, disaster is evident. The Blood of Christ has made the road of redemption a road of recovery as well. Recovery is not always easy. In fact, it's pretty painful. So many of the battles that we face in our lives; are actually battles within. I am witness that as you continue to yield to the King, those who are held captive by lies within your realm of influence are set in motion on a path to freedom. Never mind the turbulence; you must get to the finish line. Emerging militaristic prophet, your calling is not easy. Your training and development is harsh, however you were created with victory in mind. Everything you've gone through and will experience is designed to shape and mold you into the intended structure. You need every minute, second and hour of your training in order to sit in your God ordained seat of authority. It is almost impossible to engage in warfare against an enemy you don't know. As you are emerging through development you will be introduced to various levels of witchcraft, demonic hierarchy, encroached territories, and things of that nature. You will be covertly summoned to dark trenches that exist as realms, assignments, and divisions. You will meet hybrid humans on your assignments. You are being groomed to a place of resilience unheard of as you continue to pursue and yield to your destiny. My prayers are with you. I cannot emphasize enough to you the importance of keeping a wartime journal. It is expedient to your life, legacy, loved ones and future.

A LETTER TO MILITARISTIC PROPHETS

You are a precious commodity. A rare jewel embedded as the crown of creation. Your training and development has been meticulous, as you've been prepared for such a time as this. The journey has been a long and rough one. You must count it all joy. The many days and nights without understanding while walking in the spiritual dessert with the wind blowing against you in the midst of chaos and confusion, has resulted in you being formed and fashioned into an absolute nightmare to the kingdom of darkness. You have been and will continue to be processed under tremendous pressure and against fear. Keep going and never stop. It takes great courage to carry out a most daunting life assignment. You will rise from obscurity to pave the way to destiny for yourself and others for His name's sake.

You are a resilient leader.

Let submission be your official position.

~Teresa Martin

ABOUT THE AUTHOR

∽℘·℘℘

Teresa Martin is an apostolic reformer, founder of the Militaristic Prophets Institute and has mentored and coached countless prophet's, seer's and apostolic leader's through her relevant spiritual warfare and leadership courses, trainings, writings and summits. She is a leader and advisor to leaders, a sought out visionary, and revolutionary thinker.

facebook.com/militaristicprophetsinstitute.com

https://.instagram.com/militaristicprophetsinstitute

www.https://militaristicprophetsinstitute.com

https://.facebook.com/teresamartin

https://.instagram.com/teresamartin_official

NOTES

NOTES

NOTES

NOTES

NOTES

NOTES

NOTES